Streams of Influence

The Good, The Bad, and The Painful

STREAMS OF INFLUENCE

THE GOOD, THE BAD, AND THE PAINFUL

BY

ROBERT L. CARROLL, JR.

WITH

BEN CAMPBELL JOHNSON

PATHWAYS PRESS
ATLANTA, GEORGIA 30359

A Commendation

What a pleasure it was for me to read this book! I thoroughly enjoyed getting to know the author better through reading these pages, and it heightened the respect I have for him and his counseling ministry. I am thankful that he opened himself to all of us who pass through dark places. His graphic writing style holds up a mirror before all of us.

In this book Robby Carroll tells the story of how he embraced and redeemed his life experiences and how he has used them to help others in his role as counselor, pastor and friend. Having recommended many pastors to him for counseling, I can affirm that his insights and compassion, coupled with extensive education and experience, have assisted many wounded and hurting people to find peace, health and restoration. In this excellent book Robby shares with an easy style the counseling theories and methods that have impacted his own life and have shaped the foundation of his helpful ministry.

Lt. Colonel Barbara Getz
Director of Pastoral Care
The Salvation Army, Southern Territory

ISBN-13: 978-1492943488
ISBN-10: 1492943487

Copies of this book may be ordered from:

www.Amazon.com

or

Pathways Press
P. O. Box 98213
Atlanta, Georgia 30359

Contents

Preface

I am delighted that I had the privilege of reviewing and reflecting on the raw data of my life. This indeed has been an experience of a lifetime. Having someone to listen to my story, ask me questions and offer feedback, made the experience not only joyful but immensely helpful. As I reflected on my story, I saw it unfolding with all its beauty and pain. Investing myself in this rumination has enabled me to strive for both depth and integrity of life.

Never before have I had such an opportunity to awaken memories long since forgotten; this experience helped me to discover the substance of my life, the core of my essential being. As I described those vivid memories, I met diverse characters on my journey. I met a child who had been abused and was deeply troubled; I saw a compliant teenager who was sent to a boys' school and hated it; I came face to face with a fun-loving high school boy who gave life to every party he attended; I engaged a young adult who eagerly explored the world; and, I encountered a young man unable to resist the enslaving power of alcohol. This unique narrative took a new turn when I met Jesus Christ.

I hope that this very personal story will speak to multiple audiences. Many will be entertained by the strange twists of fate and their various outcomes; others will be fascinated by the power of the Spirit to transform a human life; still others will value the introduction to the numerous influences that have shaped my life. Finally, I hope each reader will find inspiration and guidance through the therapeutic insights that I have appropriated in my vocation.

I'm a seeker; I guess I'll always be a seeker. For a long time I had been seeking, but in all the wrong places. One fateful evening I discovered that the God I was unconsciously seeking had always been present with open arms to welcome me home. This Divine Presence had always been there helping me to find myself, and in finding myself to find God.

Finally, I thank Jane, my wife, for the cover art and for all that she means to me. Also, thanks to Ben Johnson, my friend without whose support and encouragement this book would never have seen the light of day.

Robby Carroll

Dedicated to
my wife
Jane H. Carroll

CHAPTER ONE

The Life of a Quester

※

YOU ARE BEGINNING TO READ MY ODYSSEY as a seeker who found! I want to open widely my seeking heart and let you see what a wounded healer passes through on the way to peace, meaning and hope. Yes!

I am a seeker and will be a seeker always until I find the elusive character who resides behind all the masks I wear.

I am a seeker and will be a seeker always until I discover what I am to do with this time that is allotted to me on earth.

I am a seeker and will be a seeker always searching for my place in this Infinite Universe.

I am a seeker and will be a seeker always looking for the ultimate goal that will satisfy this persistent yearning inside me.

I am a seeker and will be a seeker always eager to explore the mystery that surrounds me until I rest my soul in the arms of the Infinite.

What is a seeker? A seeker is a quester, a searcher, a hunter and a relentless explorer. The desire is in us, around us and beneath us; it is inescapable! We are all treasure hunters and deep sea divers on our way to the great discovery. We are seekers whether we are aware of it or not.

Is there anyone who is not looking for something? The search may be for approval, for money, for a home, for a career, for success, for security, for happiness -- any or all of these. We are by nature spiritual hunters, seekers after holy grails and pearls of great price. We are all on a quest for something which often remains nameless. When I was in the midst of my quest, not knowing which path to take, I wish that I had known two distinguishing questions to ask: For what am I seeking? And, who am I as a result of the search? The quest sounds so simple, but it is not easy because we cannot clearly identify what we are seeking. If we cannot name what we're seeking, how would we recognize it if we found it?

I once heard about a man who was drafted into the army. He also was a seeker. During his tour of duty he went about turning over papers that were face down. He found these papers in his office, lying on the ground and sometimes on tables where he ate. He compulsively turned over one sheet after another. Each time he turned over one of these sheets, he muttered under his breath, "That's not it." After three years of seeking, one day he turned over a sheet that said, "Discharged." With a loud voice he shouted, "That's it!" He knew what he was looking for and when he found it, he recognized it.

I have always been a seeker, even when I didn't know it. I sought in many places looking for an ointment to ease my ache, a light to illumine my darkness and a foundation that I could let my weight rest on. As I review my life, I recognize that for a long time I sought fulfillment in all the wrong places.

The home in which I was reared was not conducive to a young man's quest. There were too many rules, too many expectations, and certainly no reassurance and affirmation for a frightened young lad. For me to find the meaning of my life, the quest had to begin with my family of origin because it formed my earliest experience of life; there was no other place to begin. As I now realize, my parents had neither the knowledge nor the skills to help me with my life's journey. Like so many parents, they thought that if they gave me food, clothing and shelter, if they gave me an education and if they supported me when I was in trouble, which would be enough. Unfortunately, that was not enough and for too many years I fumbled my way through life worshiping at the feet of one false idol after another.

Somewhere I read the story of a young man like me who was seeking the meaning of his life. He went to a holy man and asked, "How can I find the answer to this questing spirit within me? How can I lay to rest my fears and anxiety? How can I become a true man, the person that I was meant to be?"

The holy man answered, "In every occasion ask, 'Who am I?' " All of us long for identity, but at the same time we fear the answer to the question we're asking, "Who am I?" But we must ask the question and seek the answer, or else our lives will be continually empty and meaningless.

In my teen years, finding out my identity was the last thing I wanted to do. I had a terrible fear raging within me that if I went inside and looked at my feelings and reviewed my actions and confronted my self-image, I would find nothing there. To become a real, vital, living human being requires much more than simply thinking about it; change and healing come when we confront the Self that we truly are in the present moment, and then get on the road to transformation.

In my wild and reckless days, I would never have believed that the frustration and futility of my life would actually become the ground of my calling and the creation of a new life.

Though I call myself a seeker, on my journey I discovered that I was not the initiator of the search; it was actually God who was the Seeker and the Quester for me. God was seeking me, and I didn't have the slightest notion of God's involvement with the events of my life. What I painfully experienced was fear, frustration, futility, hopelessness and helplessness. This was the stuff that revealed God's search for me, but I could not read the messages.

Much, much later in my life when I came to the end of my strength, I discovered there was a spiritual path that previously I had known nothing of. When I read the Bible, I discovered people like me who were seekers; I uncovered in the Scriptures axioms, images and parables that spoke deeply to my own condition. I want to share a few of these with you.

One day a young man, like me, came to Jesus and asked him a serious question, "What must I do to receive life, real life?" Jesus gave a challenging answer to this young man from a wealthy family who had all the security and prestige that money could buy. Jesus said very simply, "Go, sell what you have and give to the poor, and you will have treasure in heaven." Needless to say, this was not the answer the young man wanted to hear, and neither would it have been the answer that I would have appreciated.

On another occasion, Jesus was sitting at the side of a well where everyone in the city came to draw water. His followers had gone into town to get food. A woman came to this well to draw water and Jesus asked her for a favor, "Give me a drink." As a consequence of her generosity, in the conversation which followed Jesus gave her a different kind of water that quenched the deeper thirst that haunted her longing heart. This story gives hope that there might be water from a well for a parched spirit.

In his travels across Galilee, Jesus encountered a blind man whose name was Bartimaeus. This man cried out to Jesus for help.

Jesus asked him, "What do you want?"
Bartimaeus responded, "That I may receive my sight."

I mused to myself, can it be that simple? Is all I have to do acknowledge that I'm blind and cannot see and the gift of sight will be given to me? How can I find my sight?

I think I was very much like the Ethiopian eunuch who was reading the Hebrew Bible as he rode in his chariot on a wilderness road. His chariot moved along uninterrupted until he encountered a man named Philip whom God had sent to the eunuch to help him understand the Scriptures. Reading the Bible by myself was not enough for me either; I needed someone to explain to me what it meant and how I could follow its teachings.

In the early days of my seeker's life when I was making my way through the Bible, I ran into statements that Jesus made about this quest. In one of his talks, Jesus said, "Seek and you shall find, knock and it shall be opened to you, ask and it shall be given to you." To be quite honest, I didn't know how to seek or where to knock or what to ask for. I stumbled along as a seeker in the dark

Jesus told the story of a man who found a treasure hidden in a field. The man wanted the treasure, and he sold everything that he had and bought the land where the treasure was hidden. This story encouraged me to believe that somewhere there was a treasure for which I could search, but when I found the treasure, it would cost me everything.

One other thing I received from listening to the words of Jesus. One day a man came to him who could not see. Jesus made a kind of salve out of sand and spittle and rubbed it on his eyes. Jesus asked him, "What do you see?" The man said, "I see men as trees walking." Jesus touched him again and he saw clearly. This image gave me hope that finding was not a one-time affair, that for the blind to see, it took additional touches from the hand of the Master.

There is another story of Jesus that comes close to home for me. Near the entrance to Jerusalem was a pool that reportedly had healing powers. As Jesus passed by, he found a crippled man sitting by the pool. He asked the man, "Do you want to be healed?" An obvious answer came forth: Of course I do. The man explained that he had been sitting by the pool for more than three decades and nobody ever offered to put him in the pool. Right then and there Jesus healed the man.

This story for some time has been a description of my life. First is the question, "Do you want to be healed?" The answer to this question seems so obvious. Well, of course, I want to be healed. But when I think of healing, I realize it will entail walking into a totally new way of living. I know how to sit by this pool and do nothing; I really don't know how to live a different life. Healing will require an odyssey into the unknown.

As you will discover when you read my story, I have made my way through the maze of life often lost by taking the wrong turn. Slowly, ever so slowly, I began to find myself and in finding myself, I found God. Or rather, God found me. You see, seekers don't have to go anywhere to find God; God waits for them on the road of the self.

So if you ask me who I am today, I will answer, "I am one who waits for God." I am one who pursues the center of life, the core of my being. I am one who goes behind theology, creeds and dogmas to meet God, the living God. I am in search of the Light that enlightens my darkened soul. I am one who has realized that the distance between God and me is Me. To lead the life of a quester requires all of us to be aware of what we're seeking and why we're seeking it.

While I'm very grateful for the opportunity to review my life, this reflection is not for me only, but I hope also for others. In honestly sharing my own story, it is my hope that it will serve as a mirror of some of the reader's own struggles; the details of our lives are different, but the process we go through is similar. When I began this project, I did not realize how much buried material still lay in my deep memory. Reviewing these experiences has helped me to connect many of them with pain and disillusionment. This endeavor has been a maturing, healing experience for me. Though it is not necessary, I hope that some of the things I have discovered will open new vistas for you and be of help to you on your journey.

I noted the various influences and experiences that have deeply shaped who I am. Perhaps it would be better to say that I have learned ways to set free the inner person, the man in me that I could become, the person I was created to be.

Realizing that the things that have helped me might also help others, I have set forth the story of my life to discover the accumulated experiences which I am drawing from as I live my life and seek to help others. Though it came later, my conversion to Christ is the single most important thing that has ever happened to me. Christ began to set me free, give me an identity and empower me to become the person I already was.

My sense of call to the ordained ministry, followed by my years in seminary, gave me an understanding of Scripture, the church and the ministry that heretofore I knew nothing about. During my time at Columbia Theological Seminary, I took a course in pastoral care. This course inspired me to work at Georgia Baptist Medical Center for two more years, which pushed me closer to the deepest interests of my life and gave me tools with which to pursue them.

Serving as a hospital chaplain on the psychiatric ward, the pediatric unit, the neonatal intensive care unit and the oncology unit gave me an insight into people in crisis that I could not have gained anywhere else. The patients in these different sections of the hospital had different diseases, but the uncertainty and fear were the same.

Since my days at seminary, I have served the church in many capacities: as an associate minister, as the organizer of small groups and a ministry to singles, as a committee member in the Presbytery of Greater Atlanta and as a consultant to struggling and conflicted churches. Working in the church, as well as serving as a consultant to the Salvation Army, demonstrated to me that individual problems also have a social dimension and must be considered in therapy. Family therapy, for example, must include every member of the family and all their relationships.

I have had therapy from a number of very good therapists. My work with them not only brought healing to me, but revealed a methodology that was helpful in my own practice of counseling.

To these experiences, I must also add my membership in Alcoholics Anonymous and my relationship to Alanon. I know of no organization or movement that has meant as much to persons struggling with alcohol, drugs and other addictions. The principles and the methodology work in a variety of situations.

My experience in leading a weekly group of caregivers to Alzheimer patients has given me insight into a long, painful struggle and the support that loved ones need.

As a consequence of being a seeker, I have studied Ericksonian hypnosis, Neuro- Linguistic Programming (NLP) and the Enneagram, a personality profile. In addition to these approaches, I also became acquainted with Appreciative Inquiry and Celebrate Recovery, an adaptation of the Twelve Step Program. My repertoire also includes Parenting Groups, Communication Studies, Trauma Resolution Therapy, Mindfulness-Based Stress Reduction and Cognitive Behavioral Therapy for Depression and Anxiety.

All of these events, therapists and strategies have been extremely important in the unfolding of my life. These are life-giving, hope-filled strategies that create changes here and now in ordinary lives. By reviewing all of these experiences and the particular therapy that stands behind them, I will distill from this my own therapeutic approach. And, as I share these insights with you, I hope that you will be able to apply them to yourself and to those with whom you love and live.

I invite you now to begin this Odyssey by joining me as a newborn child in the strange world of York, South Carolina.

Chapter Two

Growing Up in a Southern Culture

———————————

*

I WAS BORN THE SECOND CHILD IN OUR FAMILY on March 24, 1943. I share this birth year with a number of notable people. George Harrison of Beatles fame. Bobby Fischer, the unbeatable chess player. Popular singer John Denver. Heralded American actor Robert De Niro and British actor Sir Ben Kingsley. Perhaps sharing this birth year with these famous names added very little to my life, but I like to think that some unusual and talented people were born in 1943, and I'm glad to share that year with them.

The year that I was born, the United States was in the midst of the big war, World War II. My father was away serving in the Army Air Corps and stationed in Philadelphia, Pennsylvania. While he was away in the military service, I lived with my mother, an older sister, my aunt Blanche and my grandmother on my father's side. I shared the house with this group of women who lived together under my grandmother's watchful eye.

Until the war was over, I lived in this house with all these women who referred to me as "a little man." In my earliest years of which I have only a vague memory, I was surrounded by these nurturing, caring women who supported and guided me until the war ended and my father returned home to pick up his life again. These women connected with me in alternative mothering roles; I felt loved and secure because of these relationships. When my father got home and assumed his role in the family, I had a difficult time bonding with him. This lack of early bonding with my father laid the groundwork for serious conflict with him in the years to come.

My Parents

My mother's name before she married my father was Carolyn Harriss. I have very sketchy knowledge of her mother and father. I do know that he was one of six brothers from Texas; they were in the cotton business in New York. My mother's family was very wealthy. At one time the family owned a steamship fleet and ran a cotton brokerage firm. My mother's uncle, Richard Harriss, was the president of the New York Cotton Exchange. My mother's brother, Langdon, and her half-sister, Ginny, were reared together, partly in Long Island, New York and partly in England. My mother was brought up by a governess, along with the maids and butlers employed by her mother. Her life in her early years was very different from the life that she experienced in South Carolina.

I recall her talking about a pony named Patches and a little cart in which my mother rode. I pictured her riding around Long Island being admired by all her friends. In her rearing she had been taught refined manners. Her family had strict rules about eating, meeting people and behaving with proper social etiquette. As a child she ate her meals in a dining room separate from her parents. They called her into their dining room to curtsy and bow to guests. My grandfather on my mother's side died when my mother was eight years old. After his death she and her half-sister, Ginny, were sent to England to a Catholic boarding school to finish high school.

My grandmother went to England each summer and rented different castles where the family spent the summer together. My grandmother was married four times and seems to have had a hard time establishing a lasting relationship. From all that I have heard about her, I believe that she was manic depressive. After suffering from depression for a good many years, she committed suicide. After my mother finished high school, she moved to Washington, D.C. to live with her mother and her stepfather, who was a Spanish diplomat. At that time my mother attended a finishing school just outside of the city.

When her mother committed suicide, she was sent to Greenville, South Carolina to live with one of her uncles. This uncle lived on an estate in the country outside the town. Through her move she met my father.

My father, Robert Lindsay Carroll, was born in and grew up in York, South Carolina. He was one of five children, three boys and two girls, who were twins. From my observation, it seemed that his childhood was quite different from that of his siblings. For openers, he had a serious stuttering problem. An impediment like this has a devastating effect on one's self-esteem, and it also creates a variety of the reactions from one's peers. Another contrast between him and his two brothers was in their educational experiences. His brothers were both high achievers; they both were college graduates -- one from Davidson College and the other from the Georgia Institute of Technology. His twin sisters graduated from Winthrop College in Rock Hill, South Carolina. My father attended the Citadel and the University of South Carolina but graduated from neither. From all that I have heard about him, he seemed to be quite a loner when he was growing up. These differences from his siblings and his parents' perception of him undermined his sense of security and place in the family.

His mother and my grandmother, Blanche Lindsay, attended Converse College in the 1800's and was herself a high achiever. So he was surrounded by educated, accomplished family members. My father was not ignorant or mentally inferior, but I believe that he suffered from a significant learning disability coupled with his stuttering problem. As a consequence, he acted out his frustration as a child by yelling and throwing temper tantrums. The family lore was replete with stories about his being a bad little boy who was always getting into trouble. Later as a grown man, he did the same.

When my daddy and mother met in Greenville, he was working in a cotton mill – the penalty for not having an education. Carolyn and Robert were the most unlikely couple to end up with each other. My mother had been raised Roman Catholic, my father Presbyterian, so they compromised by being married in the Episcopal Church. (As you might imagine, my father refused to agree that his children would be reared Roman Catholics.) As a child, I heard many times about the gigantic wedding they had at the Christ Episcopal Church. Photographs recorded the grandeur of a fine, high-class and very expensive wedding.

My mother's family was quite certain that she had married beneath herself by attaching herself to an uneducated man working in a cotton mill in South Carolina when she had been a celebrated debutante in Long Island, New York.

This description makes it obvious that I was born into a family representing two very different cultures -- different outlooks on life, very different ideas about manners, customs, traditions and norms. My father came from a typical family that honored southern traditions and emphasized maintaining close family ties. My mother, by contrast, had never been part of a close family. She was reared by governesses and hired servants, sent abroad for her education and lost her parents early in life. She never learned to cook because maids did this kind of work in her family. She had no need to develop cherished southern cooking skills. My father, on the other hand, was a great cook and had never been catered to by servants.

As a result of my mother's rearing and her expectations, I sat at our dining room table listening to her explain the importance of the proper use of a fork, a spoon and a knife. I learned that a salad fork is for eating a salad and a regular fork is for eating the main course; I learned which spoon was for soup and which one was for dessert; I learned the difference between a table knife and a butter knife. In this new territory of upper-class culture my father began to pick up these cultural niceties and practice them. In fact, he became even stricter than my mother about the use of proper utensils. Once when I picked up the wrong spoon to eat a bowl of ice cream, my father's face turned red with anger and he screamed so loudly about that spoon that in my child's mind I thought the walls of the house would cave in on top of me.

The relationships in our home were filled with other undercurrents. My father had an enormous amount of anger which he could unleash in a moment. I think my mother also was frightened by his unpredictable rage. Another source of anxiety in our family relationships may have resulted from the demand for total respect of authority and how this demand was enforced. This applied especially to respect for women.

One day I was playing in the front yard when my mother came to the door and said, "Robby, it's time to come in for dinner."

I said, "Okay, mom, I'll be there in just a moment." In less than a minute, the front door flew open and my father came running into the front yard where I was playing. He grabbed me by the collar and took me back into the bedroom and whipped me with his belt. He told me never to tell my mother that I would be present in just a moment. From that experience and others like it, I developed an irrational fear of authority.

That experience of rage and punishment defined my dominant relationship not only with my father but with all authority figures. I was convinced that my father really did not care about what I thought or desired. It appeared to me that he only cared about himself and his desires. That encounter resulted in my making a character-shaping decision. At that early age I decided that my father did not desire to communicate with me to work through our differences. Working out conflicts and misunderstandings had no place in his list of priorities. I have seen the image of my father in many other persons who are hotheaded and overreact to the least of things.

In later years I've often pondered what it felt like to live in such an unstable environment. In the evenings we usually sat at the dinner table in the dining room eating on fine china with elegant silverware and linen napkins in our laps. A person passing our house and looking in the window would have thought us to be an ideal family. We were anything but ideal. As I sat at that table, I was filled with dread. I never knew when I would be blasted with anger for something I had done or not done. As I recall those scenes, I realize how I often bowed my head and gulped down my food. As I packed in the food, I ate for comfort rather than for nourishment. Driven by anxiety and fear, I gained weight. Often I found myself hoping and praying that a friend would invite me to have dinner with him and his family so that I could escape my family table.

My parents had a daily ritual of gathering in the kitchen to make dinner and pouring drinks of hard liquor and glasses of wine, which doubtless helped fuel the tension at the table. Having drinks daily before and during dinner was a fixed tradition in our home. By the time we sat down to eat, the anger, judgment and overreaction to the smallest of things scarred me as a child. I later recognized that both of my parents were highly functioning alcoholics. No child ever knows what to expect from highly functioning alcoholics. He cannot guess how they will react to a given situation. This destructive behavior created in me the belief that in conflicted relationships, I could not speak out and seek to resolve the battle. The responses that I would have received for my effort would have been criticism, ridicule and sarcasm.

On one occasion my father began criticizing me. I sought to explain to him what I was doing. Then I said to him, "Daddy, I am sorry." He replied repeatedly: "Oh you're sorry; oh you're sorry; oh you're sorry. How could you be so stupid?" Experiences like this convinced me later on that only within the context of unconditional love and acceptance can human beings grow and become mature. This hyper-judgmental environment in which I was unable to question my parents about anything stifled my emotional growth and development. Emotionally destructive environments like this cause nothing but pain and illness, and they mar the life of a child.

As I have reflected on my story and have spoken with my two sisters about my life journey, I realize that our experiences of family life were not the same. My older sister is three years older than I, and my younger sister is five years younger. Our ages, gender, birth order and the changes that went on in our family at various points in our lives make our stories dissimilar. As a Marriage and Family Therapist, I often see that siblings from the same family of origin can have very different experiences. As you read my story, I hope you will be able to identify with and affirm whatever your life journey has been. It is in speaking our truth to ourselves and each other that we find healing.

York in the Summer

Though I suffered a great deal of anxiety in my family environment, there is also another side to my years in York. Once I turned my mind toward those early years, I had a flood of memories about that period. I was born and lived in the home of my grandmother until we moved to Greenville. Even after we moved, I spent some of my weekends and summers in York. I still can see through my mind's eye that big three-story house that had no central heating or air conditioning. It was my job to bring in kindling from the woodshed and coal from the coal bin to place in the fireplaces around the house. I had to keep them properly supplied and stoked. In the yard there were always chickens and cats running around looking for a way to brave the winters. We called my grandmother Maamaa. I idealized my Maamaa. She was a kind, caring, soft-spoken woman who was proud of me and encouraged me to be my best. For years she taught the Women's Bible Class at the First Presbyterian Church.

On Sunday mornings the women's classroom was filled with big wicker rocking chairs occupied by the class members. The ladies sat around in those rocking chairs, wearing their large hats with pins in their hair buns. In her teaching my grandmother was elegant and persuasive as she stood at the front of that class teaching them about the God who spoke through the Bible. After Sunday school and church we returned to Maamaa's house for Sunday dinner. The maid, whose name was Grace, always had a big lunch prepared for us. Grace worked for my grandmother for many years; I don't remember a time when Grace was not working for Maamaa. In her relationship with Grace, she was unconsciously affected by the racism woven into the fabric of the culture which seldom received critical evaluation.

Treatment of Blacks

My grandmother, a highly respected Sunday school teacher and leader in the town, had Grace working for her for many years. Grace's two-room house, which my grandmother owned, had dirt floors and no running water; the toilet was an outhouse in the backyard. I sometimes went to that little house and visited with Grace and her family. This fine Christian woman, my grandmother, truly believed that these accommodations were good enough for Grace and her family. Racism was an invisible demon that in those days held captive much of the south. For example, the African-Americans in York were required to take a written test on American history if they wanted to vote. I can still close my eyes and see a line of African-Americans waiting at the courthouse in downtown York. They stood or sat waiting to take the test hoping to gain the right to vote in the next election. It's hard to believe today that such blatant discrimination was acceptable behavior for the general population, even Christians.

Shopping for Groceries

On several occasions, I went grocery shopping with my grandmother; we usually did our shopping at the York Supply Company. Maamaa and I would get in her old car, which, when she cranked it up, sounded like an airplane with no mufflers. I can still hear that whirling sound of the motor as the car backed out of the garage. Chickens and cats ran in every direction to get out of the way of this noisemaker. When she pulled out of the driveway and turned toward King's Mountain Street and toward Up Street, everyone cleared the way for Maamaa.

After a few blocks we turned right on a dirt road that led to a back alley of downtown. She parked the car and we got out and walked through the back door of the York Supply Company. The store was long and narrow with counters down the middle aisle. There were multiple lights hanging from the ceiling over each counter. As we entered, the voice of the owner came ringing through the store, "Hello Miss Blanche, hello Miss Blanche, welcome." Miss Blanche was a respected member of the community; she walked around the store and pointed out to the owner all the items she wanted. Everything she pointed to, the owner boxed up and set to one side. When we returned home, his deliveryman, an old African-American, brought our purchases on his mule-drawn wagon; the clippity clopping sound could be heard up and down the street. He turned into our back driveway, unloaded the groceries and stored them in the pantry.

As I recall the delivery, the last thing he did was to take ice tongs, grasp a large block of ice and place it in the ice box. My grandmother did not have an electric refrigerator; nobody did. The ice box served the purpose of a refrigerator, but it had to be cooled with a block of ice every few days. At least once a week, a new block of ice was placed in the ice box to keep the food from spoiling. In those days no one had anything like a modern-day kitchen stove; the stove was fired with wood. The only light in the kitchen was a single light bulb hanging down from the ceiling just above the table. Grace filled the wood stove with kindling and paper and lit it with a match. The fire built in the morning was kept going all day for cooking both on top of the stove and in the oven. The stove also had elevated warming closets where leftover food was kept. Grace opened these little doors and put food in the warming closets to keep it warm until it was served and then stored the leftovers in the warming closet until supper.

Later in the day after breakfast, many a time I went into the kitchen and grabbed a biscuit out of the warming closet. This biscuit with butter and jam was a treat that I often enjoyed. Those memories of being in

York with my grandmother are filled with graciousness. She loved me with an unconditional love. That unconditional love and acceptance which she offered to me did not extend to Grace and her family in the same way. Today, I am ashamed of my failure and that of my family with respect to Grace and other black people. Anyone would have had to live in that culture to understand the unconscious grip of racism on our daily lives.

I loved summer vacations because it meant that I was able to spend time with my grandmother. My first cousins, Walter and Mason, also came down from Conneaut, Ohio to spend the summer with Maamaa. They were twin boys about my age. Generally, we spent the night on the third floor of Maamaa's house. One night around midnight or 1:00 a.m., we were awakened by strange noises. We were scared to death. In those days we believed in ghosts, and we especially believed that there were ghosts in our grandmother's attic. The sound of footsteps running back and forth on the roof kept us awake and filled our hearts with terror. We jumped out of bed and ran down the narrow staircase leading to the second floor and to our grandmother's room. When we got to her room, all of us jumped into her bed screaming, "Maamaa, Maamaa, there are ghosts in our room."

She calmly got out of her bed, walked up the narrow stairway to the third floor with us and sat on the edge of our bed listening and waiting for the ghost to walk. When we heard the noise again, our grandmother said, "Boys, these are not ghosts but squirrels running back and forth on the tin roof." We were disappointed because we were at an age where everything seemed to be mysterious and magical.

In addition to my cousins, I had another good friend, Johnny Spratt, who also lived in York. I loved playing all day with Johnny and we both loved swimming, especially in the Flemings' pool, just up the street from Maamaa's house. The Flemings owned the local movie theater and lived in a beautiful house on top of the hill. In the backyard they had a large, beautiful swimming pool. They were always very generous in allowing the neighbors to come and swim in their pool.

The Flemings had a son who was a little older than Johnny Spratt and me. His name was Tommy, a weird sort of guy. He had several chemistry sets that he hid down in the woods behind the house. We explored the woods with Tommy and watched him mix up concoctions with his chemistry set. When those concoctions belched out smoke that dissipated among the trees, we often wondered if one of them might explode.

Later, when we got older, I heard that Tommy had gone into the real estate business with his mother. Apparently their relationship was not going too well. One day Tommy returned to his mother's house with an ax in his hand. Evidently, he was hiding behind a tree when she approached the house. As the paper reported the story, he ran at her with the ax and pounded her to death. What an unbelievable tragedy. I couldn't imagine this weird little boy becoming a violent man who could chop up his beautiful mother with an ax. Weeks after murdering his mother, Tommy was put on trial. His father begged the court for mercy, claiming that Tommy was ill and should be placed in the state mental hospital. The judge acquiesced to his request and placed Tommy in the state asylum for the mentally ill. I never really knew what became of Tommy and his father, but the story still haunts me.

I cannot think of York without recalling that it was one of those small southern towns where everyone knew everybody's story. All the residents knew who were the town's movers and shakers; they knew the town drunk and the mentally challenged guy who roamed the streets. Hours and hours were spent talking about all the happenings in town – who was seeing whom, who was giving the biggest party and who had the most money. Many summer days we sat on my grandmother's porch, drank iced tea and talked about all the people in York. Our conversation always included who was sick, who died, who was getting married and to whom and who had a new baby. All the town gossip was shared on that porch. Gossip helped weave the fabric of the culture and keep everyone in their respective places. I think this was really my first encounter with group therapy. Everyone talked about everything and everybody.

CHAPTER THREE

Life in Greenville

✳

WHEN MY FATHER CAME BACK TO YORK after the war, we moved to Greenville. We lived at 408 McIver Street. Our neighborhood had many children my age. Some of the kids that I played with were Artie McCall, Gil Gilreath, Joe Byrum, Sally Thornton, Pat McKinnon and Johnny Pettit.

Boyhood Exploits

One day Gil and I teamed up to make some money. Concurrent with this idea, we heard that the circus was coming to Greenville. The circus always pitched a large tent on a vacant lot and covered the ground with sawdust which served as the floor. As we approached the big circus tent, there were sideshows all the way up to the entrance into the big tent.

Inspired by the circus, Gil and I decided to put on a sideshow for the younger children in the neighborhood. We got cardboard boxes, filled the bottom of the boxes with dirt and put strings along the top of the boxes. We then went out to the garden and caught caterpillars, hundreds of them, and filled the boxes with leaves and caterpillars. Once we had everything set, we went throughout the neighborhood barking out invitations to the Caterpillar Walk. Our message to the other kids was come and see the Caterpillar Circus. All the little children who showed up had to give us a nickel just to peep into those boxes to see caterpillars walking across the strings. P.T. Barnum was certainly right when he said, "There is a sucker born every minute." We delighted in showing these caterpillars to all those little children, and to this day I have no idea how many nickels we collected from the Caterpillar Circus.

The success of the Caterpillar Circus gave us an even bigger idea. Gil's family and my family had home movie projectors, and we had small reels of black and white cartoons. Gil's house had a large, hot attic – a perfect place for our venture.

We set up the screen and the projector; we popped popcorn and filled it generously with salt. We then iced down a lot of Coca-Colas. We ran through the neighborhood waving our signs shouting, "Come to the movies at Gil's house! Come to the movies." On the day of our opening, a long line of little children stood there waiting to come in and view the movies. We collected their dimes and nickels and took them up to the attic. Our innovative strategy was to give them without charge popcorn that was filled with salt. The popcorn was free, but the drinks were a nickel. We figured the free popcorn would help us sell more drinks, and it did! Even today the memory of these entrepreneurial ventures reminds me of wonderful fun times in my boyhood. Gil and I remained friends all through grammar school and then played football together on the Greenville High Red Raider team. Gil was one of those special friends I will always remember.

Another bold experiment came when we were in grammar school. We put together a bicycle-riding circus. We built ramps to ride over and jump our bicycles, just like those cyclists in the circus who jumped over ramps on their motorcycles. We had a ball building ramps of all sizes. The first time I ran my bicycle over the big ramp, I had no idea how important it would be for the handlebars to be screwed down tightly. I got a long way back from the ramp and started riding my bicycle as fast as I could. I went faster and faster until I hit the ramp and was immediately airborne. I expected to land on the back wheel as the motorcycles did at the circus. But unfortunately the front wheel hit the ground first, the handlebars gave way and I flipped over the handlebars. After my impressive jump I went rolling like a bowling ball across the yard.

Why the teachers permitted us to set up the ramps, I have no idea, but they allowed us to put on a bicycle-riding exposition at recess at the Donaldson Elementary School. We tied ropes to the ramps and dragged them behind our bicycles the three quarters of a mile from our home to the grammar school. We proudly set up our ramps on the Donaldson playground. In our minds we pictured this as a triumphant occasion when we would be heroes and all the girls would swoon as they watched our glorious jumps time after time after time. In our imagination we could already hear the shouts of adoration from the crowd. I think it was at this time that I wanted to go into showbiz.

Nurture from Unexpected Places

Two of the most nurturing persons in my early life were Gladys and P.D. Meadows. P.D. was a large man who smoked cigars and wore a white straw hat. P.D. owned a candy factory which was fun to visit. He also had a chauffeur and two maids to assist his wife with the housework. I have a picture of myself sitting in the back seat of P.D.'s Cadillac with Cliff, his chauffeur, driving us out to the candy factory. No other eating event competed with going to the candy factory with P.D. When we arrived at the factory, he took me back to the candy line. I stood there as the chocolate turtles and other fascinating candies passed by on a conveyor belt. P.D. encouraged me to take some and to eat all I wanted of these fine candies.

Gladys and P.D.'s granddaughter, Pat McKinnon, lived with them. She had numerous friends, and their house was open to us all. On Friday nights we gathered at Gladys and P.D.'s house not for candy but for music. Pat had a 45-rpm record player and all the popular songs of the day. As fifth and sixth graders we played those records and shag danced until late in the evening. Often Cliff, the warm and friendly African-American chauffeur, shared the singing, dancing and eating with us. He was a kind man and loved and cared for each of us children.

Cliff and the other African-American men who worked in the neighborhood were the kindest men I ever knew. They treated us kids with love and respect as if we were their own children. One day Cliff was standing in the front yard of P.D.'s house looking very sad. Gladys was in the hospital quite ill. With tears in his eyes, Cliff began talking with me about Miss Gladys. I can still hear his high-pitched voice praising her and expressing just how much he loved her. While we were standing there talking, he prayed for her to get better. Seeing such emotion expressed in a man was a rare experience for me. Clearly Cliff was filled with compassion for Gladys and was not afraid to show it. That day I did not realize what an example he was setting for me. He displayed the traits of caring, openness and empathy that I longed to have for others and longed to receive from those close to me.

Grammar School in Greenville

My years in grammar school were fantastic for me socially, but a very difficult time for me academically. When I entered the first grade at Donaldson School, my teacher was Miss Baxley. She was a stern woman who established rules that left no doubt about who was in charge in her classroom. As I sat in her class being terribly homesick, I wanted my mother to come and get me. I didn't like school and didn't want to be there. Reading, writing and arithmetic were miles over my head and completely beyond my comprehension. From my first day I was placed in the slow, slow, slow reading group. Because of my poor skills, I never enjoyed reading. Reading assignments were particularly hard for me. I know that I created trouble for many of the teachers because I was so unhappy with myself and my performance in the classroom. My teachers in grammar school were trouble for me, just as I was trouble for them.

In spite of all my struggles to do acceptable work, there were still a few good times even at school. I was chosen to run the movie projectors in the auditorium where the whole school gathered. When we had an assembly, I got dismissed from class early to set up the screen and the large movie projector. Perhaps the teacher was glad to get me out of her room for just a few extra minutes. At any rate I delighted in my job because I felt needed and had a sense of belonging.

I also remember with pride being chosen to be a patrol boy. The distinguishing mark of patrol boys was a white shoulder band with a badge attached to it. This decor wrapped around my hips and my chest. Morning and afternoon we stood at the corner and helped children cross the street. The school patrol also got to march in the Christmas parade. In that notable event we formed a line immediately in front of the float on which Santa rode down Main Street in Greenville.

My favorite teacher in grammar school was clearly Ms. Lide, my sixth grade teacher. In addition to being in her class, I periodically went to her home for tutoring. She always showed patience with me as a struggling young boy; her responses to me gave me a feeling of acceptance in spite of my conflicts. She realized that I had trouble reading as well as excelling in my other subjects. Reading was always difficult for me, and that complicated learning in other fields of study.

In school I also developed a number of satisfying relationships with my classmates, which I very much appreciated. At school I took pride in the fact that I was popular with most of the students and had many close friends. Our football team at Donaldson Elementary was coached by a woman. Having a woman for a coach was an unusual arrangement when I was a student. Our team had uniforms and cheerleaders just like the senior high team. We held daily practices on the playground, and that was much like our recess. At practice and at recess we threw the ball around and chased each other endlessly. Our practices were filled with chasing, running, tackling and even fighting. In my early years it was perfectly acceptable for little boys to get into pretty fierce battles on the playground. The teachers seemed to think that some of us who were rowdy in class could work out our mischievous classroom behavior by slugging it out on the football field. I seem to remember that fighting was even encouraged. So in football practice we took out our aggressions in an organized rather than a disorganized manner.

Pawleys Island in the Summer

In the summers of my grammar school years I spent many weeks at Pawleys Island, South Carolina. Some of the people who lived in Greenville spent their whole summer vacations at Pawleys Island, which is between Charleston and Georgetown on the coast of South Carolina. Many of the people who vacation there are old and brown from the sun, wind and sea. One of the descriptions of Pawleys Island on a bumper sticker read: "Pawleys Island -- Arrogantly Shabby." Unlike modern beach houses, those on Pawleys Island have no air-conditioning and very few amenities.

For several summers my friend Bomer Smith came to the beach with us so that I had someone to play with. He and I spent many hours in the creek behind the beach house fishing, gigging and seining. Bomer and I got up early in the morning, went to the creek and pulled our seine through the water. In short order we caught hundreds of tiny, creek shrimp. We seined until we had enough shrimp to feed the whole group of vacationers at our house.

At night we waded through the creek with gas lanterns and gigs. A gig is something like a fishhook, only larger, and it was used with a stabbing motion to catch a fish. On the bottom of the creek we found flounders buried in the sand. An interesting thing about flounders is that both eyes are on one side of their head. We gigged one flounder after another. That creek was teeming with marine life, and we had a gleeful time harvesting seafood and taking it home. Our relatives all cheered when we walked in the door hauling our treasure of shrimp and flounder.

On Pawleys Island we always had a local African-American maid who did the cooking. She and the other cooks lived on the mainland, and in the morning they picked up food to cook for the summer visitors. These seasoned women chefs were experts at cooking hush puppies, seafood and cheese grits, all things that we Southerners loved.

The African-Americans who were reared in this part of South Carolina were a rare group. Their skin was so black it was purple. Their language was Gullah, an English- based Creole language. I had to listen closely to decipher what they were saying. They entertained us with many stories of the ghosts that roamed the beaches on Pawleys Island. The most famous of all the ghosts was named "The Gray Man." It was said that "The Gray Man" walked up and down the beaches of Pawleys just before a hurricane was to hit the island. I have many heartwarming memories of those days during which we watched for the "Gray Man" and where we spent our time swimming, fishing and playing in the sand, a good tonic for a little boy's soul.

One day as we were out seining in the creek, we discovered the bow of a boat sticking up out of the sand. We were amazed! It was an old wooden boat mostly buried and appeared that it had been that way for years. We began digging until we unearthed it and immediately gave this water-soaked, resurrected boat a name, "The Orphan." We gave it this name because it had been orphaned in the creek so that it had to be found and rescued. The rest of the vacation we dragged "The Orphan" behind us in the creek as we seined for shrimp and gigged flounders. "The Orphan" was a perfect place to put our nets and the buckets filled with our catch.

One day we had a brilliant idea, at least it seemed brilliant to us. Bomer and I decided "The Orphan" needed a sail. We went home and daddy created a giant sail made from oil cloth. We erected it in the middle of the boat and were convinced that "The Orphan" was now seaworthy. A few days later, we decided to push the boat across the inlet at the south end of the island and sail it out into the ocean. We pushed and pulled until we finally got "The Orphan" to the ocean. Now we were ready for the ocean cruise.

Our family gathered on the beach – my father, mother, sisters and a few of the neighbors who lived in a house near ours. Our plan was to launch "The Orphan" into the ocean and sail down to Retreat Beach, which was the beach north of Pawleys Island. Unfortunately, my father thought we said that we would sail down to the north end of the island. He was expecting us to come back to the beach when we reached the north end. By the time we got to the north end of the beach, we were at least a mile out in the ocean. We were sailing with glee in our newly resurrected and refurbished boat. While we were cruising, my father, mother and the neighbors were all running up and down the beach waving their arms trying to get us to come in to shore. They called the Coast Guard and reported the danger that the youthful sailors were in. While we were having a howling good time, they feared we would be lost at sea.

Finally we reached Retreat Beach and got carried in by the waves as we sailed gently onto the beach. As we pulled "The Orphan" up on the beach, we looked out toward the ocean and there was my father in a little motorboat boat yelling at us. When he got within a short distance, he screamed, "What in the hell are you all doing out in the ocean on that water-soaked skiff?" With panicked fear we swam out to the rowboat and hopped in with my father, whose rage and angry accusations continued to flow unabated. He turned the little motorboat around and headed back towards Pawleys Island. When we entered the North Inlet, he shouted to us to get out of the boat. We were afraid and pleaded, "Daddy, there are sharks in the North Inlet; please don't make us get out." He kept yelling, so we got out and swam to the island while he returned the rental boat. I will never forget that memorable cruise on "The Orphan"; neither did my father, nor my friend Bomer.

As I look back on those grammar school years, I recognize that everything was not good, but neither was it all bad. I had academic problems when I went to school. I know that my ability to learn was in many ways affected by my home life. When anyone is anxious about himself and wonders how the adults in his life feel about him, it is difficult to concentrate and learn. Also, I have wondered if I had a learning disability that went undetected. This would seem to account for many of the struggles that I had with school. In spite of the academic challenges and my home situation, I found many things for which to be grateful and also many ways to have good fun.

CHAPTER FOUR

Sent Away to Boarding School

---

*

I THOUGHT GRAMMAR SCHOOL IN GREENVILLE WAS CHALLENGING, but it was nothing compared to boarding school. After finishing the seventh grade I endured an experience that significantly impacted my life – I was sent away to a boarding school. This was not of my own choosing. A few mistakes and failures led to this terrible time in my life. This downhill skid gained momentum after the automobile wreck.

When I was a budding teenager in South Carolina, we got our driver's license at fourteen years of age. After successfully getting my license, one day I was driving down Augusta Road and one of my friends was lying down in the seat beside me. I glanced over for just a moment, at which time the driver of the white car in front of me slammed on his brakes. Not reacting quickly because of my distraction, and perhaps driving too fast, I hit the car and caused a serious accident. When the police came, they contacted my father. This accident was the last straw. My father was fed up with my misadventures. Not knowing how to rear me and what I needed, he decided to send me off to boarding school where someone else had to deal with me. He began looking into schools that I could attend and he could afford; he found an all-boys school in Arden, North Carolina. It was Christ's school in name only.

Christ School was founded in 1900 by Thomas and Susan Wetmore. It is an all-boys boarding school in Arden, North Carolina, seven miles southeast of Asheville. It has a 500-acre campus with about 200 students. This school was only loosely affiliated with the Episcopal Church and received no funding or direction from the denomination. The chapel at the school was the longest continuously operating Episcopal Church in western North Carolina.

I went to Christ School when I was fourteen years old. Actually I had finished the seventh grade in Greenville but when I enrolled at Christ School, I had to repeat the seventh grade. So in the fall of my fourteenth year I arrived at Christ School as a boarding student. I was scared, homesick and confused. On the first day I spent at the school, I walked out on the football field where I sat down behind some tall bushes on the track which surrounded the playing field. After I hid in the bushes for a time, I began to cry and cried and cried until I could cry no longer. I do not remember a time that I felt so forsaken and alone. My boarding school experience began in tears and got worse.

The seventh graders were called brats by the upperclassmen. As the youngest boys at the school we lived in a dormitory with two senior boys in charge of our behavior. Their handbook listed all kinds of punishments for breaking any of the rules. There was to be no running in the halls, no food kept in your room, no being late getting into your room after lights out. Other directives included making up your bed, sweeping your floor and keeping your room orderly. The list of rules touched every possible thing that could go wrong, and the punishments were extremely harsh, especially for the brats.

The seniors who were in charge of our hall had large wooden and fiberglass paddles. The punishment for running in the hall, for example, was five licks with the fiberglass panel. My roommate, Dexter Christenberry, was from Knoxville, Tennessee; he and I were the largest seventh graders on the hall. One night the two seniors who were our monitors came into our room after lights were out. They ordered us to stand in the middle of the room and start slugging it out with each other. They ordered us to spit on each other and then slam each other in the face. Dexter and I were very close friends. It was painful physically and emotionally for us to beat each other up. For some idiotic reason the senior boys wanted us to entertain them by acting like we were gladiators. As I reflect on this bizarre incident, I conclude that when you cage a bunch of men or boys together, meanness, hatred and aggression flourish. My first year at Christ School was a very difficult year in my life, to say the least.

Mr. Dave Harris, the headmaster of the school, proudly proclaimed that Christ School built men, whereas Asheville School for Boys, another school across town, built gentlemen. What he meant by building men was teaching them to fight, beat and abuse other little boys to make men of them. As I look back on this experience, I realize that my father went to the Citadel at a time when hazing was in full swing. He and I both were immersed in a culture that believed abuse built character and honesty in little boys.

The yelling and screaming at the dinner table and the beatings my father gave me for relatively minor offenses were abusive. The administration at Christ School took this abuse to a new level; they believed such punishment helped a young man function better in a competitive culture. But this abuse convinced me that I was bad, seriously flawed and stupid. My father had over and over repeated to me that I was stupid, and I was beginning to believe him.

Other School Experiences

Though school primarily came to mean failure and punishment, there are some positive memories from my years at Christ School. As part of our learning the students did all the work on the school's dairy farm. One of my jobs was attending a coal-fired furnace in one of the dormitories. The coal came to the campus in a large boxcar on a coal train. The boxcar was parked on a side track next to the storage space. These coal cars did not open at the bottom so that gravity could draw the coal into a storage bin. Rather, it was necessary for us to get into the coal car and shovel the coal into a truck parked on the side. Hour after hour shoveling coal, one shovelful at a time, into that waiting truck was hard work for a young teenage boy. This strenuous job taught me to develop a "whistle while you work" attitude. I became so convinced that I even began to enjoy shoveling coal into the waiting dump truck. I can see that seventh grader now on a cool, fall day, with the leaves turning orange and red on the mountainside around him, shoveling coal into a dump truck – shoveling coal, singing and whistling. This new habit helped me go to a different place in my mind and find joy in a difficult situation.

I had a few other good experiences at Christ School. One year a friend of mine from Greenville, Teddy Wagner, came to Christ School. We joined in a bit of mischief together. As I have indicated, the school had a rule that you could not have food in your room. If students were caught with food, they were assigned a stump to dig.

As you might have surmised, my friend Teddy was caught with a box of cookies hidden under his bed. After the inspectors found this contraband, the disciplinarians announced that Teddy would be given a stump on the property to dig up. Because Teddy was my good friend, I told the Student Council that the cookies were mine. I came forward and stated to them, "I will take responsibility for digging up this stump." With delight, it seemed to me, they gave me the largest one they could find, a huge oak stump that must have been four feet in diameter. I spent the whole football season digging it up.

I was not allowed to have any help with the digging. Through that experience I learned how to use axes, shovels and mattocks. As I dug deeper and deeper around that stump, cutting each root one by one, finally after three months I was able to separate the roots from the stump so that it could be pulled from the hole. What a sense of accomplishment I felt when I finished that task because I previously had no idea that I could dig out a four-foot stump. I learned that I could work through even the harshest of punishments.

Another experience at Christ School that I deeply treasure is having a job for two years as a kitchen boy. There I came to know in a personal way the kind, caring and joyous African-American cooks. One of the cooks was a large, unusual man named Theodore Roosevelt McDaniel – we called him Pete. He was always unselfishly gracious to me and to everyone who came his way. He stood behind that huge dishwasher dumping plates into a barrel underneath the table. When the barrel got full, he took it out to slop the pigs. As he worked, he whistled and sang and smiled and his behavior toward me caused me to feel deeply loved and accepted. I realize today that my experiences in childhood with men that gave off warmth, love and acceptance came from African-American men rather than white men.

Other cooks I met included an African-American couple whom we knew simply as Julius and Elizabeth; I never knew their last names. Julius was as skinny as Elizabeth was round. And, oh how they loved me! They called me "sugar" because I was responsible for going down a narrow staircase to the basement below the kitchen and bringing up hundred-pound bags of sugar to fill the sugar containers on the tables. I liked the name "sugar." Much of the time Julius sat over in the corner telling jokes, smiling and laughing while Elizabeth did all the work in the kitchen. Julius seemed to hold the title of "king of the kitchen" while Elizabeth soldiered on with the work that had to be done.

Julius was more of an ornament than a worker; he sat on that stool wearing his white chef's hat, his white apron and his perpetual smile. At the same time Elizabeth seemed glad to do all the work and protect Julius from having to lift a finger. Pete, Julius and Elizabeth were the kindest people I met at Christ School. In that kitchen I learned that those who are less favored in the culture are often the ones who show the most love, compassion and understanding. Those who are highest in the ruling order seem lost in competition, climbing the ladder of success and taking control. I may be speaking too harshly of those in power, but there was quite a difference between my experience in the kitchen and my experience in the classroom and on the sports field.

Certainly my time at Christ School was a mixed bag. Although much of it was painful, it was at the same time extremely valuable and part of what I appreciate in my life journey. Although I would not send my child to a place like Christ School, I have learned in part how to value this difficult challenge. I learned a great deal about self-reliance and how to deal with adversity. As a brat I experienced what it is like to be at the bottom of the pecking order, and I also witnessed how immature people in positions of power and authority can abuse others. This lesson taught me what I did not want to be: I did not want to lord it over others. I pray that respect and care will guide my steps through this life.

CHAPTER FIVE

Senior High and Beyond

✳

THERE IS NOTHING LIKE A HOMECOMING! My father had demanded that I spend four years at Christ School, so after I finished the tenth grade I was free to return to Greenville. From the time I was a child, I had idealized being a student at Greenville High School. As a child I went to nearly all their high school football games. I attended a special event that always took place on Thanksgiving Day – the game between Greenville High and Parker High. Virtually the whole city participated in this highly anticipated event. Most of the people in Greenville who worked in the mills had children who attended Parker High. The kids of the mill owners and mill executives generally attended Greenville High. The Thanksgiving Day game not only was a battle between the two schools but also between the two cultures – workers and owners. On Thanksgiving Day on that football field, young men played out either their anger or sense of superiority generated by the conflict between the two cultures in this southern mill town. The setting for this social battle took place at Sirrine Stadium, the football stadium of Furman University in Greenville.

After returning to Greenville from Arden, with all my positive feelings about Greenville High, I registered and showed up for football practice with the Red Raiders. On the first day of practice in the middle of August, it was hot and humid. Before practice started, I sat alone in my car while other fellows who knew each other milled about visiting, laughing and renewing friendships. Because I had no connections, I felt lost and alone. I felt like an outsider; I yearned to be a part of the culture of the team and the school. Finally, practice began and I got out of my car and walked slowly to the locker room. I went in and changed into my uniform. Practice began with running laps on the track that circled the football field.

In that era coaches had not realized that players could work out in shorts and T-shirts. We all were dressed in pads and long pants. The heat and humidity sapped all the strength and energy out of me. I was a fat little kid struggling to make just one lap around that track. The coaches kept yelling at us to push, push, push as we struggled with the laps. I had such a deep desire to fit in and to be included that I was willing to go to any lengths to become part of this team.

Finally, the day of scrimmage came. I knew that to make a place for myself on the team I needed to hit and slam as hard and as loud as I could. I knocked my teammates to the ground because I wanted to demonstrate that I had what it took to play for the Red Raiders. With all the effort that I was putting forth, it was not long until I was included and began to feel part of the team. After a few weeks my teammates nicknamed me Spanky. I knew that the nickname was a badge of belonging and I wore it with pride. I was looking for any assurance that I was beginning to be part of the right crowd.

At Greenville High we had fraternities and sororities. I was a member of the Thalia Club. Soon I was elected vice president of the Thalia Club, which carried with it being the social chairman. One of my key responsibilities was organizing and running initiation for new members. Initiation consisted of paddling, beating and other forms of hazing. The first year that I was in charge of the initiation, I recalled the pain and humiliation that I experienced from my hazing at Christ School. Because of this vivid memory, I announced to the Thalia Club that hazing would be discontinued. This was a very unpopular stance to take, and I knew that I was using a lot of my popularity capital to take that stand. But I saw no value in putting people through an abusive initiation to become a part of the club. We did have an initiation that year, but it did not include hazing. As I think back on this decision, I realize that my own experience of being hazed created an understanding that prohibited my sponsoring it. There is no value in beating, intimidating and putting down human beings in the name of making them better or well adapted for membership in a club.

One of the distinctions of the Thalia Club was that no alcohol was allowed at our parties. There were other clubs whose members consumed a great deal of alcohol. Motivated again by my deep need to belong and be admired by my classmates, I hung out with guys who did a lot of heavy drinking. This decision to search for popularity and a sense of belonging began my own fall into alcoholism. My idea of self-control consisted of drinking until all the alcohol was gone. Those of us plagued with this disease seem to have no capacity to stop; we will continue to drink until we pass out or get stopped by someone like a policeman.

As I look back on my high school days, I see a mixed bag of experiences. On the one hand, my family life was difficult from the beginning and throughout my school career. I felt unnoticed, unappreciated and rebuffed on numerous occasions. My negative experiences with classes followed me through grammar school, Christ School and high school. I was a young man who was motivated to gain acceptance and popularity at any price. My struggles with academics, my lack of self-confidence and my yearning for acceptance created a fertile field for alcoholism to control me. Perhaps it is a minor miracle that I survived all of this.

I realize now that in those years I often felt out of place but if the truth were told, I had many friends and was elected as a Senior Superlative in my graduating class. I was chosen as the wittiest boy in the class. I was also chosen as the most valuable member of my high school fraternity two years in a row. I recognize that sometimes achievement is driven by an underlying sense of insecurity, but that was not my emotional driver. I do not think that I was particularly insecure. In ministry and as a therapist I often see folks who, though they are driven by fear, have become experts in disguising their fears and insecurities.

Discovering the Big Wild World Beyond

After my junior year in high school, I had a life-changing experience. I began to explore a different world and to experience myself and my needs in a totally new environment. The changes began for me the summer after I finished the eleventh grade. My older sister, Lynn, and I traveled together throughout the major cities of Europe. Our mother signed us up for a ten-week trip that included ships and trains and good hotels. Mother and daddy drove us to Montreal, Canada where we boarded the ship for England. The ship went up the St. Lawrence River and down the St. Lawrence waterway and across the North Atlantic to our destination. When we landed in Liverpool, I looked out of the window of our ship and saw the coastline. What an amazing experience! I had read about England with its rocky coastline, but somehow I didn't realize that it was actually there. Now, here I was on board this ship, looking at what I had previously only read about.

I began to realize that there were people just like me beyond those beaches, and they had never heard of Greenville High School and the amazing Red Raider football team. The trip over on the ship had been for me one glorious party. The bars were always open. There were good-looking women walking around the ship everywhere I turned. Together we drank and sang and danced. On board the ship there were festivals like dress-up parties to which I can remember wearing a toga and an ivy leaf around the top of my head. At that party, I got drunk as a skunk. I don't recall ever getting out of bed before 1:00 o'clock in the afternoon. The cruise over may have been the best part of the whole trip. I wondered why anyone would fly when they could sail on a ship like this and drink liquor and have parties all the way. It was a blast!

After we disembarked, we began our tour of London. I remember the Tower of London, the British Museum, Hyde Park, Buckingham Palace and Westminster Abbey. We stayed at a hotel that was just off of Hyde Park. I had heard about the popularity of pubs in London. We visited a pub called "Dirty Dicks," a historic pub built in 1745. We spent a great evening there drinking and eating fish and chips. How different this was from the pinball machines and jukebox beer joints of Greenville. It was a beer joint with class. The experience blew my mind. After a few days in the United Kingdom we crossed the English Channel to the continent, which gave us the opportunity to visit the major capitols of Europe: Paris, Rome, Brussels, Amsterdam, Copenhagen, Oslo and Stockholm. In all these centers of culture and tradition, we visited the impressive cathedrals and spent hours in the art museums. I could feel my perception of the world changing: the earth is huge, it has people everywhere, and what has happened in these lands has been the substance of the world's story. I think that it is impossible to travel and absorb experiences like these without being expanded in understanding and vision. My mother, who had done a great deal of international travel, knew that this would become an epoch-making part of my education. She was loving and caring in her desire to expose me and my sister to the multi-faceted world in which we live.

When I returned to Greenville, how could I ever explain to my friends and relatives what had happened to me? Quite honestly, it was difficult to share these new ideas with any of my peers. I feared that they would judge me, thinking that I was bragging about my different perceptions of life and the world or underscoring my position of privilege in the Greenville community. Whether I desired it or not, this extended trip, plus my going away to Christ School, really did set me apart from my peer group. I had experienced much in life that none of them had, nor would they ever. When I realized that having explored the world was a part of my mother's identity, I began to have a deeper understanding for the society from which she had come and the richness of her upbringing. I began to identify with her just a bit more when I considered what it meant for her to be reared in a wealthy family who could send her to a convent school in England and a finishing school in Washington, D.C.; I could not help but feel closer to her and grateful for her vision. Moving to Greenville and marrying did not destroy her appreciation for an informed, cultured, expansive life.

Some Failed Starts

During my senior year in high school it was clear to me that I was not ready for college. In fact, I did not even want to go to college. Based on my conclusions about college, I, along with two friends of mine, joined the naval reserves. In 1961 and 1962 we attended weekend training at the Naval Reserve Center in Greenville. After my graduation from high school I boarded the Southerner, a train of the Southern Railway, and headed for the submarine training school in New London, Connecticut.

In the summer of 1962 after completing the rigorous training at the submarine school, I returned to Greenville. In a few weeks I was to report to Charleston, South Carolina to board a submarine and fulfill my assignment. On the way to Charleston I had to stop in Columbia to

47

have a physical examination before going on active duty. Much to my dismay I failed the physical and was given a medical discharge from the U.S. Navy. Missing out on the naval experience was quite a shock to me and also a grievous disappointment. I had looked forward to serving my country with my two friends who joined the Navy with me. I was quite surprised that I did not pass the physical because I had passed all the physicals prior to joining the Navy and entering submarine school. The doctor flunked me because of my weight; I didn't understand this because I had been overweight all my life and that had never stopped me before. I went back to Greenville with a deflated spirit.

I then returned to Greenville and in the spring of 1963 I entered the University of South Carolina. I realize now that I was still motivated by a deep desire to belong. When the fraternity rush started, I threw myself full speed into rush week. Every night that spring semester I was out drinking and carousing with fraternity members. I had good friends from Greenville who belonged to different fraternities, and I oscillated back and forth trying to decide which fraternity to join. When I received bids from both the Sigma Alpha Epsilon and the Kappa Alpha fraternities, it was quite a dilemma for me to decide which to join. After bids had been made, all the pledges to the various fraternities showed up in the middle of a field in the midst of fraternity row. One at a time we ran to the fraternity house that we had decided to join. Among cheering crowds of people who watched the pledges choose a fraternity and run to the house, I struggled with my decision. I decided for Sigma Alpha Epsilon and following that decision I continued a semester of partying, drinking and celebrating with my fraternity brothers.

Not all of our partying was done on campus; we sometimes left Columbia and drove to the beach on Wednesdays, cutting classes and returning to the university on Monday. Since I spent most of my time partying and drinking, when the final day of the semester arrived, I had four F's and a D in my classes. Needless to say, the Dean's office advised me not to return in the fall.

Lost and confused about what would happen next, in the summer if 1963 I returned to Greenville to again live with my parents. As I explored options, my father told me that I could go to Greenville Tech and major in drafting and design technology and he would then give me a job with his company. Since I had no other open doors, I signed up for a two-year course in which I studied machine and architectural design. I continued to drink and party just as I had at the University of South Carolina. I had never enjoyed going to school, and the technical school was no different.

After graduating from Greenville Technical Center, the highlight of those wandering years came in the summer of 1965, when I decided to join with a group of my friends who were going to Oregon to work for Pendleton Frozen Foods. I was assigned the task of driving a truck. It was an exciting experience driving across the fields in Oregon picking up loads of peas that had been harvested. As I was looking for the field that I had been assigned for that particular day, I reveled in the beautiful landscape. I pulled the large truck into the field which was filled with migrant workers picking peas. The farmers had huge combines that went through the fields shelling peas, putting them in a container and blowing the vines out on the field. The migrant workers picked up the baskets of peas and dumped them into a large bin. As I pulled up in the field, I got out of the truck and mounted a tractor that was rigged with a forklift and loaded those large bins of peas onto a flatbed truck and transported them to Pendleton Frozen Foods.

Working at Pendleton Frozen Foods provided me my first exposure to migrant workers. They lived in long, dormitory-style houses erected in the fields. These houses were filled with bunk beds where everyone slept – they included both men and women in the same house. I couldn't converse with these workers because I spoke no Spanish and they spoke no English. To communicate we simply made hand motions. The workers were always pleasant and welcoming as we worked together. As I look back on this time, I realize that I lacked an understanding for what these migrant workers were living through every day of their lives. As I see it today, they were experiencing a form of slavery.

After working about one month in Oregon, I had an opportunity to go to Alaska and work with a crew of fishermen. I was excited about this new adventure. I left the fields in Oregon and went to Seattle where the fishing boat was docked. The King Crab boat was in dry dock in Seattle being repaired. The skipper of the boat, along with his son and the cook, were working together to get the boat prepared for the next trip. Daily I joined them in sandblasting, painting and repairing the boat. Our task was to repair the boat and make it ready for the long journey up the inner passage and across the Gulf of Alaska towards Kodiak and Port Wakefield. Once we arrived at our destination, we would fish for king crab. The inner passage was impressive, breathtaking and awesome with its beautiful scenic landscape on either side.

On the way to Kodiak, we stopped at Ketchikan. The buildings, people and activities made it feel like we were in the Old West. We tied up to the dock, got off the boat and walked down the street to a bar in the center of town. As we walked in, I noticed the floor was covered with sawdust; at the bar men in cowboy hats and jeans sat drinking bourbon. I immediately pushed my way to the bar and started drinking too. The bar was a replica of saloons I had seen in countless Western movies, and I felt like I was back in the Old West drinking with live cowboys and pioneers.

When we left Ketchikan and continued up the inner passage to Kodiak, our skipper decided to take a shortcut across the Gulf of Alaska to Kodiak. He made this decision knowing that the Gulf of Alaska was famous for having the roughest seas in the world. As we crossed the Gulf, we got into a heavy, heavy storm. The waves must have been twenty feet high, tossing this little fishing boat up and down as we crossed the Gulf. Unfortunately, the spillway to the crab tank at the back of the boat had been left open. When we started taking on water, the bilges of the boat began to fill up and a warning bell rang. It rang and rang in the middle of the night after all of us were asleep. When we went down into the engine room, we saw water waist deep that could eventually sink the boat. With water still pouring in through the attached spillway, Don, the skipper, went down into the engine room and reached under the water trying to repair this pump. If he did not repair the pump, the water could not be pumped out of the engine room and the boat would sink.

Two of the crew members were seasick, lying like dead men underneath the table in the galley. They were so sick that they didn't care what happened next. Don, his son and the cook were working hard to save us all from this tremendous storm. The skipper, his son and I were hauling buckets of water out of the engine room and up the stairs – one tiny bucket at a time. The cook dumped the water overboard in what seemed like a hopeless effort to keep us from sinking.

Don kept at the task of making the pump effective again. He

was one of those farm boys from the Midwest who knew how to fix anything. He had grown up on a farm where there were no mechanics to call when something happened to a tractor. Through trial and error Don learned how to do everything to keep machinery running. He was fantastic with his hands. This ability to fix things on a boat is exactly what it takes to be a king crab fisherman in Alaska. The Coast Guard could be days or weeks away when you are in the midst of a storm. Waiting that long would result in a sunken ship and dead crewmen. I am glad that Don had the skills and the determination to fix the pump and save the ship and all of us on it.

Our guidance for navigation was done by triangulating radio station towers to determine our location in that vast ocean. Navigation was much more complicated in 1965 than it is today. Finally, we arrived in Kodiak; we were all overjoyed to step out on dry land. One of the traditions of arriving in Kodiak was to break out a case of Canadian Club whiskey that Don had purchased in Seattle. We each got a bottle of whiskey and went to the local bathhouse; we sat in a steam room eating, drinking and celebrating our arrival.

Again I felt like I was right in the middle of the Old West sitting in a hot tub telling great stories of how we had avoided death on the high seas. The next day we left Kodiak to go to the small port of Wakefield. Wakefield Fish Company was the company to which Don sold the crabs that he had caught in the Gulf. At the fish company the workers loaded the large king crab traps on the back deck of our boat. After loading these traps and adjusting the rigging, we set out into the Gulf. Don seemed to know just where to drop the traps to catch crabs. We baited the crabs with plastic bags which had been punched with ice picks and filled with bits of fish. The smell of fish in the plastic bags leaking out through the holes attracted the crabs to the traps. What an exciting moment of anticipation when we pulled up these traps to find them filled with crabs.

The next day we made the rounds pulling up crab traps. The back of the boat was rigged with a hydraulically driven wheel that pulled up the rope attached to the crab trap and hoisted it onto the back deck. As traps came up filled with crab, they were dumped on this deck. Of course, some of the traps had very few crabs in them, but others were filled with king crabs. These king crabs look like giant spiders with a small body and very long legs. After we pulled them up, we had to measure each crab with a template to determine if it was large enough to keep. Each time a trap was dumped on the deck, we ran quickly with the template measuring the crabs, picking them up and either tossing them overboard or into the crab tank.

When we got a full load of crabs, we returned to Port Wakefield and unloaded them onto a waiting processing ship. In 1965 Wakefield Frozen Foods paid ten cents a pound for king crabs. Ten cents was a lot of money in the 1960s when gasoline was thirty-one cents a gallon. As a worker on the boat I received room, board and $20 a day. That meant I made $140 a week with no expenses because all my meals and lodging came with the job. For a kid who flunked out of the university and did not have a job, $140 per week was big money.

Another vivid memory that occurred in the Gulf of Alaska came as a mishap on board the boat. When we were dropping crab traps into the Gulf, I was climbing up on top of the traps to untie them one by one and throw each one overboard. As I was walking from the front of the deck along the side of the boat, the huge stack of traps started leaning towards me and I could feel them beginning to press on my body. I thought that I would be crushed between the side of the boat and the heavy traps that were about to fall. Skipper Don was driving the boat and he saw what was happening. In a flash he quickly turned the wheel to starboard and gunned the engines, forcing the traps to lean in the opposite direction, thus saving me from being crushed. I was amazed at the quickness with which he sized up my situation and took corrective action that saved my life.

I could characterize this period of my life as a series of failed beginnings. In my last year of high school, I had enrolled in the navy and after my training was rejected for active duty. I attended the university for a semester and flunked out. The only way open to me following this underachievement was a course in design at a technical school. This path was quite short and I ran away to Oregon and eventually to Alaska, where I made good money but could have lost my life.

These misadventures left me with little confidence in myself and no vision for the future. At this point I could not imagine that there was any value or meaning in the failures that I had suffered. Still not knowing what to do, in the fall of 1965 I re-entered the University of South Carolina and this time I paid more attention to my studies because I had to pull up to a B my four F's and a D.

CHAPTER SIX

Seeking Life in the World of Religion

---

*

WHEN I WAS A LITTLE BOY, I attended church on a fairly regular basis. We went to Sunday school and Sunday worship. I have warm memories of sitting beside my grandmother in church. I also was active in the youth fellowship at church as a teenager. For me there was, however, always a disconnect between church and the rest of my life. Although we attended church, it was not a centerpiece of my life nor of my family's. The people that I knew at church shared my social life. Church for me was one of those habitual things that you simply did whether or not you knew why. I do not remember anything from sermons that were preached, and I must have heard a hundred or more. I really did not understand what the preacher was talking about. The whole worship service and the classes went over my head.

For example, I remember wondering what the big deal was about communion. They passed the trays of bread and juice down the pews, while the organist played funeral music. Everyone sat quietly with somber expressions on their faces. I just did not get it. It appeared to me that this was a tremendously significant moment for the people in our church, but it did nothing for me. Church had no direct connection to my life; it was mostly irrelevant. When I say these harsh things about the church, it may not have been the church's failure as much as my own.

There is a story of Jesus that encompasses what I am seeking to explain. In the fifth chapter of St. John we read this story: Now there is in Jerusalem near the Sheep Gate a pool, which in Aramaic is called Bethesda and which is surrounded by five covered colonnades. Here a great number of disabled people used to lie—the blind, the lame, the paralyzed. One who was there had been an invalid for thirty-eight years. When Jesus saw him lying there and learned that he had been in this condition for a long time, he asked him, "Do you want to get well?" "Sir," the invalid replied, "I have no one to help me into the pool when the water is stirred. While I am trying to get in, someone else goes down ahead of me."

Like this lame man who came to the pool every day, I went to church every week. I sat there, as did he, and nothing happened to me. Like the crowd that milled around him, there were church members who brushed shoulders with me, but they never helped me understand why we were there. I needed someone to help me into the pool of knowledge and awareness. Nothing happened to me spiritually until I had an encounter with my inner darkness that like a nightmare awakened me from my slumbers. Perhaps it is always God that must awaken us!

The prelude to my beginning to take church seriously came in the form of a horrifying experience in the spring of 1972 after both Jane I had graduated from college and we had moved back to Greenville. At the time we were living in Greenville and I was working for the Dealer Supply Company. The day that this shock came to me stands out in my mind quite vividly still today. I was getting together with friends in Greenville who shared my drinking habits, and we decided to go to the Carolina Cup. The Carolina Cup is a steeplechase that draws from 30,000 to 40,000 people annually. The steeplechase is held at the Springdale Race Course which is situated on the outskirts of Camden. There Mrs. Marion du Pont Scott bred, reared and trained racehorses. She had a horse farm in Virginia as well as the acreage in South Carolina. In 1983 Mrs. Scott died and deeded the 600-plus acres of the Springdale Race Course to the state of South Carolina with the caveat that the land remain solely for equine use in perpetuity. The Carolina Cup, held in Camden each year, is referred to as South Carolina's largest cocktail party.

We were staying with some friends in Columbia for the weekend.

55

The night before the Carolina Cup I was drinking liquor, smoking pot and having a frolicking good time. Suddenly, without warning, I was filled with fear and a frightening experience of emptiness. I was convinced that I had committed the unpardonable sin. I knew that I had been a sinner beyond description and was convinced God had withdrawn the divine spirit of Love from me. I was terrified. I feared that I would spend the rest of my life trying to distract my mind from this terrible fate of being damned.

I remember standing up and rushing out the front door into the street. Jane followed me and stood by me. I began to sing all of the hymns I could recall. I recited all the scriptures and prayers that I could bring to mind. I was frightened and I was weeping. Jane came to my side to comfort me, but there was no comfort for me in my distraught state. The Carolina Cup was no longer important, as I was feeling the darkness and terror of being damned forever. I felt driven to get to our home in Greenville that night. I drove all the way home with Jane at my side talking to me, seeking to soothe my soul that was sinking farther and farther into the darkness. I do not know what I would have done without her confident help. I remember Jane's presence with me, confident of her faith and love of God and me. After this frightening experience that awakened me, Jane and I began a serious life in the church.

Seekers find God in many different ways and for often conflicting reasons. For example, some people come to God in a gradual, evolving manner; others find God at the end of their long journey of seeking; a few are frightened by hellfire and damnation preaching; others, like me, are thrust into the inner void that feels like one is in everlasting darkness and eternally falling through space. With that event I was left with a head full of questions and a slight emerging hope that I could find my way to God.

My serious experience with the church began in the First Presbyterian Church in Greenville. Jane and I remember with gratitude a visit from the minister of First Presbyterian Church who had done our wedding in 1968. We were living in the guest cottage beside the swimming pool at my parents' house. We were in our bathing suits when Dr. Neuman Faulkner showed up to welcome us back to Greenville and to the church. We began attending Sunday school, church and a

Wednesday evening Bible study. When Dr. Faulkner retired, Dr. Randy Kowalski was called as the senior pastor.

I can't talk about my call, my training and the churches that I've served as an ordained minister without beginning at the beginning, when my life was changed through a dramatic experience that I was not consciously seeking, nor did I particularly want it. Seemingly, I had no choice in the matter, but an amazing change came in my life for which I will be eternally grateful.

One of the early experiences that I had at First Presbyterian Church was a Lay Renewal Weekend, an event that helped me get more deeply engaged in the life of the church. A few months after the Lay Renewal Weekend, my pastor and I were returning from a retreat up in the mountains just beyond Greenville. My pastor, Randy Kowalski, and I were riding back through the mountains in my red convertible. We were flying down the mountain as I was trying to give Randy a thrilling ride through the mountain passes. All the way down the mountain Randy seemed not to notice my driving, but he kept talking to me about becoming a deacon in the church. It was hard for me to hear him talk about my being an officer because I could not imagine doing such a thing. Why in the world was he asking me to serve as a deacon in the church? After a great deal of discussion during the days that followed, I agreed to have my name put in nomination to become a deacon. In many ways that decision was the beginning of a significant journey towards larger leadership in the church.

My wife, Jane, and I served as youth advisors in the church. We assumed the leadership with youth at a time when there was no youth minister in our church. Despite that fact we had a vibrant and alive youth ministry that brought forth vibrant and alive teenagers. We were also serving on the committee of Young Life in Greenville. In our church the number of Christian friends was growing like kudzu vines, and all of us were committed to share the good news of Jesus Christ with young people and older people alike. We put on musicals at the church with the young people; we conducted retreats at the Young Life Retreat Center at Windy Gap, North Carolina. We sang, prayed, shared fellowship and played together over the retreat weekends. Prayer was a transforming part of the retreat program. The new life that burst forth on the retreats, we sought to nurture when we got back home.

I have a vivid picture in my mind of Wednesday nights when the youth room was filled with kids sitting on the floor with the lights dimmed praying aloud to Almighty God. What an amazing power we experienced through the Spirit of God! Those young people with their depth of faith and their eyes upon Jesus Christ taught me lessons in living the life of a disciple of Christ.

Those early days of my Christian journey in Greenville were formed by my engagement in the life of a vital church. The church reformed my faith and my picture of the world, a picture that would be tinkered with when I got to seminary. I wonder why I went to church for thirty years before I found out what church was about!

As a new Christian I was a serious seeker. On Sundays I watched Oral Roberts on television conducting those unbelievably marvelous healing services. People who could not walk came forward in wheelchairs and crutches, received an anointing and prayer, and then threw down their crutches and danced across the stage. This all happened when Oral prayed for their healing. For quite some time Jane and I immersed ourselves in Oral Roberts' teaching on Seed Faith. His preaching in those years revolved around Seed Faith – giving what you had and expecting God to bless it four-fold. Seed Faith encouraged us to open our lives and offer our talents as resources for God's use. In response to his message, we offered ourselves as fully as we could to God. I now look back on that time with both gratitude and confusion. Later I began to suspect that the Seed Faith Movement was a fund-raising effort for his ministry or an investment rather than a service. I still appreciate the spiritual emphasis on giving in confidence that God will reward our efforts. Jesus had promised, "Give and it shall be given unto you."

Another aspect of my call came to me when Randy Kowalski appointed me to the committee studying the mission of the church. We met once a week for an entire year searching the Scriptures and discussing the mission that Christ had given the church. At the end of that year the committee made a proposal to the session of the church that we embark on a Lay Witness Ministry as an expression of our mission to other churches and the denomination. With great enthusiasm we moved forward with that lay witness program.

These experiences provided the basis for confidence that eventually led to my decision to attend Columbia Theological Seminary in Decatur, Georgia. Some Sundays I sat in the pew observing Randy Kowalski preach as he led the worship of Almighty God. As I listened to him preach, something moved deeply within me. The voice within was calling me to do what I saw Randy doing – preach the gospel. Being called by God was an amazing experience for me because I did not think of myself as an orator or public speaker. Not only did I stutter, but I made below average grades in school. I had never been a student. I could not imagine that I would or could be a preacher. After participating in the lay witness mission work, I gained confidence in the call that God was offering me. Some days I could confess that God was calling me to ordained ministry. In the weeks and months that followed Jane and I struggled with whether or not God was calling. Should we or should we not go to seminary? We had two little children, a house and a job. Jane had come through a significant period of depression and hospitalization. Her doctor strongly advised against our leaving Greenville to go prepare for the ordained ministry. He said, "The worst possible thing that you could do to Jane would be to enroll in seminary." We later found that Jane had suffered from postpartum depression.

As I reflect on these days, I am deeply touched by the faith of my wife. When she was emerging from a period of struggle with depression, she was saying "yes" to my decision to go to seminary. She said "yes" to that decision in the face of her doctor telling her that this was the worst thing for us. Jane has been on this journey with me from day one. Her faith, her honesty, and her struggle with life continue to be a source of inspiration to me. This story of my conversion to Christ after a near-emotional breakdown remains a great marker in my life. The report that I have given regarding my pastor, the lay witness mission involvement and the clues that I have pointed to regarding the call, do not tell the whole story. This testimony does, however, make the seminal points of my engagement with God and the amazing way that the Spirit worked in our lives. As I survey the whole experience of call, the one lasting gift to me has been deliverance from alcohol.

This deliverance from alcohol was something that I could not have done alone. Bill Wilson, the founder of AA, discovered that the only way he could get sober was to share the journey to sobriety with someone else. We lived in a culture where cocktail parties and wine and beer were a part of everyday life. Drinking was a part of every family and social gathering. I could certainly see that my drinking was out of control. It was my wife's dedication and kindness that made all the difference to me. She offered to give up alcohol with me. Jane saw that I could not do this by myself, so she suggested joining with me in what was a major life change.

Jane's support in creating a new life that did not include alcohol was a key to my recovery. I can remember the joy that I felt taking walks in the evening, being able to connect and have meaningful conversations with Jane. I began to enjoy the freedom and the richness of life that alcohol had somehow prevented. I felt more alive and present to others and to life without my abuse of alcohol. I became more open to spiritual and emotional natural highs. I truly experienced New Life. To experience something new, I had to give up something old that was holding me back.

Nothing else could have remained had I not found release from this powerful, demonic force. Of course, the next move was from Greenville to Atlanta and my entrance into Columbia Seminary.

CHAPTER SEVEN

Life at Columbia Theological Seminary

———————

�֍

AFTER MY LIFE-CHANGING EXPERIENCE OF CHRIST, I became more and more deeply committed to the Christian mission. I participated as a Sunday school teacher, youth advisor, deacon, Young Life Committee member and Lay Renewal team member. More and more I was feeling the call to ministry and receiving encouragement from others to consider a full-time Christian vocation. Jane and I went to Atlanta for a weekend to explore the possibility of joining the Young Life staff. Later our minister, Randy Kowalski, took us to visit Columbia Theological Seminary. This was a serious time of prayer and discernment. After this initial visit to Columbia, we attended an Inquiry Weekend at the seminary.

Attending this weekend event was a good experience that helped me to understand what seminary life would be like. During the weekend we attended a class, met other people who were seeking to discern their call and visited in a professor's home. After our exposure to Columbia, we made the choice to explore my call by enrolling in seminary. From that weekend on, we began making plans to attend the seminary in July. For juniors (first-year students) entering the seminary the semester did not begin in September but in July at Greek school. The first course I took in seminary was Koine Greek, the Greek of the first century.

First Presbyterian in Greenville was a conservative church built on the foundation of a conservative interpretation of the Bible. Among the members there was no question but that the Bible was the Word of God spoken to us through various writers who were inspired by the Holy Spirit. When I got to Greek school, the first thing I heard was that there were variant readings of these ancient texts. Variant texts referred to different words and phrases and sometimes a paragraph in the oldest manuscripts. I learned that the ancient manuscripts had been copied by hand, and occasionally one of the scribes added in the margin a comment about the text and the next scribe included his comment in the text. What did this information do to the belief that the Scriptures were inerrant, the Word of God as God spoke it through the writers of the Bible?

The acknowledgment of these differences in texts said to me that this Bible might not be the Word of God; it has been corrupted by men. When I considered this, I had a sinking feeling in my heart. I thought to myself, "I've sold my house, quit my job and moved my family to Decatur, and the Scriptures with all these variant readings may not be the Word of God." I had believed that the Scriptures were the inerrant Word of God and instead of being the inerrant Word of God there were hundreds of variant readings. What was I to believe? This first experience in Greek class clarified to me why the members of my church had cautioned me not to lose my faith at seminary. As I continued my study that first year, I learned that understandings of Christian beliefs, traditions and practices are as diverse as the human experience itself.

Frankly, I was frightened by what I was learning in seminary because it was so different from the religious culture I had grown up in. This shocking awakening was the beginning of a journey that was extremely difficult for me intellectually, spiritually and emotionally. Everything that I believed when I went to seminary was challenged, and I was forced to rethink the foundation of my faith. It took the better part of a year for me to realize that these godly professors had been placed in my life to teach me the knowledge and skills that a minister required. I nurtured the fragile belief that God had put them in my life to help me broaden my perspective on the Christian faith. Finally, during the first year of classes, I was able to open myself to learn and grow under the tutelage of these dedicated men and women.

As I began my journey toward ministry and counseling, Jane grew and developed as an artist and poet. She has studied for many years with a number of notable artists. She spent a summer at the Artist Student League in New York as well as several times of study in Philadelphia to study with Nelson Shanks, a renowned portrait artist. Jane has published four art and poetry books and has several hundred pieces of art in collections throughout the southeast including portraits, landscapes, still lifes, figures and drawings. Her first two publications were placed in the governor's library collection. Recently, Jane was chosen to exhibit her art in the executive offices of the Governor of Georgia.

A common thread running through our marriage is that we are both passionate about our diverse fields of endeavor. We enjoy a synergy inspired by the other's work and growth. I have learned that one of the most important things that a couple can have in marriage is a shared vision. Our vision is that we are both committed to and supportive of our own, our families and each other's growth and development. The piece of art that Jane has on exhibit with the governor is "Family of Blossoms."

As I look back on my early experiences in seminary, I now recognize that I really did not know what the new life in Christ meant. In the early stages of my training I could not anticipate how I would be opened to the universality of God's love, God's compassion and God's understanding of all people, not just those who were like me. It began to dawn upon me that the grace of God in Jesus Christ was beyond my understanding. While I experienced the grace of God in the depths of my soul, it lay beyond my capability to put this belief into words. Though men and women spend years writing systematic theology, in the end it is impossible to capture the grace and compassion of God in words. Perhaps Christ came to show us this reality in the flesh because it could not be captured in words.

At the time that I was struggling with these issues, I took a course in "A History of Christian Doctrine" with Dr. Catherine Gonzalez. She is a compassionate woman filled with great faith and a strong confidence in the gospel. She stood before our class and spoke of the great spiritual figures in Christian history as if they were her next door neighbors. As she spoke about their lives, beliefs and practices, it seemed that she knew all of them personally. She understood in a profound way what they had struggled with in their lives on earth and the insights they had bequeathed to us. They, too, had to learn to follow Jesus Christ in their time just as I had to learn to follow him in mine. I realize now that as I made my way through seminary, I was changed not so much by what my professors taught as by who they were.

I took a class from Dr. Gonzalez on the "Theology of Schleiermacher and Kierkegaard." The highlight of the course came for me the evening that she invited the whole class over to her home for dinner. She and her husband Justo, who wrote our text on "A History of Christian Doctrine," prepared for us a Cuban feast of black beans and rice. That evening as we discussed the writings of Kierkegaard, we focused not so much on his theological concepts but on his idea that purity of heart was to will one thing with your life. In a small book by Kierkegaard, Purity of Heart, we were challenged by the haunting truth which we again engaged after dinner. That discussion made me realize that I was double-minded and had always been so. I find it exceedingly challenging to will one thing and one thing only. This profound insight which we discussed in class took on new meaning when we sat informally in the living room after a good meal and conversed about world-changing ideas and how they challenged our lives.

Another positive experience that I had at Columbia Seminary, which supported me through many changes, was a relationship with my advisor, Theron Nease. Everyone in the seminary called him T. Nease. During my time at Columbia he struggled to get his Ph. D. dissertation finished, went through a divorce and later discovered that he had prostate cancer. He and I got together for lunch at least once a week. He often shared with me how isolated and alone he felt among his colleagues. It seemed to him that his fellow professors distanced themselves. He wondered if they felt he was unclean because of his renegade nature and lifestyle. Our relationship was different. In it I experienced a great deal of love, compassion and understanding. I saw him as a real man who struggled with real sin.

Two memories of decisions that T. made stand out above the others. Although he was divorced from his wife Judy, when he found that he had cancer and had a very short time to live, he contacted her and remarried her so that she could get the benefits of his church pension.

If he had died divorced from her, she would have gotten nothing. I judged this a kind and caring thing to do. Even in death he was thinking about securing support for his ex-wife and his children.

On another occasion when he and I were having lunch together, he spoke of the brevity of the time he had to live. He grabbed his arm and said, "Robby, this flesh is going away; this flesh is dying." "The thing that gives me hope," he continued, "is that somehow my investment in life will live on through you and others whom I have taught over the last twenty years." What an intimate, connected and meaningful experience this relationship proved to be! I found through this renegade seminary professor a sense of intimacy that I had longed for.

My relationship with T. was an antidote to the isolation and loneliness that I had felt so often in my life. Here was a man who believed deeply in the grace of God through Jesus Christ; he was also a sinner saved by grace. He spoke fearlessly of his failings and of his love for God in Christ. In his life and imagination these two great truths belonged together. What a blessing to have someone with whom I could celebrate the good news of Christ without restraint! I think part of my appreciation for T. came because it stood in such contrast with the conservative, evangelical community of my origin. As deeply as I loved all those brothers and sisters, we were not able to be as honest as I had experienced honesty with T. Nease.

Another professor at Columbia, Dr. Ben Kline, was one of the most knowledgeable, patient and stalwart souls that I have ever known. A graduate of Yale University, he was a brilliant scholar in Philosophy, Theology and the Bible. In addition to being brilliant, he was kind, compassionate and understanding. When I took my first philosophy course from Ben, I came to the class as an uneducated, immature student. I was both frightened and confused with what philosophy had to do with the preaching of the gospel. What did philosophy have to do with God? Ben Kline, in a gentle, patient way, led me through the history of the great philosophers and helped me see how they gave us tools to understand the gospel today. He gave me a variety of ways to see the world, ways to engage God in the events of our time and how to work for God with a biblically informed heart. He helped me connect the dots between the various world views, the ways we engage with God and how the Bible fits into every issue of our lives.

Ben was not offended by my stupid questions. He was not offended by anyone's questions. One day in class when a student asked him a particularly deep and difficult question, he raised his right hand, placed it on his forehead, closed his eyes and held it for several minutes. When he removed his hand and opened his eyes, the wisdom flowed from his mouth. As I continued to listen to him, I recognized that he was investing all the intellectual gifts that God had bestowed on him to enrich the lives of all of us.

After I graduated from seminary and was working in the church, Ben was always available to help in difficult situations. When I called him, he graciously invited me to come to his office and converse with him about issues and struggles that I was having. Later in my ministry I was working with a congregation that was going through a particularly difficult time. They were concerned about a change of ministers, and the issue had created a severe division within the congregation. The Presbytery asked me to meet with their session. I had been engaged with the church for about a year when I invited Ben Kline to conduct a seminar to help us understand Presbyterian polity with respect to the congregation. His seminar clarified the situation and helped us move past the places where we were stuck.

Another significant experience in seminary grew out of the practical application of ministry. I spent a summer at Smyrna Presbyterian Church in Conyers, Georgia as an intern working under the guidance of Rev. Carl Smith. Carl's story is unusual and quite interesting. He came to seminary under the "extraordinary clause," which allowed people who did not have a college degree to get seminary training. In his early life Carl had been a tractor dealer in South Georgia. He was a big, heavyset man full of good will and laughter. He also had the reputation of being the most conservative minister in the Presbytery of Greater Atlanta. Though he wore the conservative label, Carl was the most gracious, uncluttered man that I have ever known. He invited everyone from fundamentalists to conservatives to liberals to speak in the Smyrna church. I learned from Carl much about being open to all people.

One of the highlights of my experience at the Smyrna Presbyterian Church was participation in the annual camp meeting. The camp meeting was held in a big, open-air sanctuary called "the tabernacle."

At each corner of the tabernacle there were large water coolers where people gathered before and after worship to drink lots of water to get relief from the hot summer sun. When it came time for worship, the tabernacle filled with people, and old-time gospel singing got underway. I recall the pianist at the front of the tabernacle banging out the hymns on the piano. I can still hear those people singing at the top of their voices those great old gospel themes – Amazing Grace, Bringing in the Sheaves and I'll Fly Away. The music and the singing were really the best part of the gathering.

Carl invited preachers from all around the south to preach at the Smyrna Camp Meeting. The sermons were long and strong. The preachers tended to go on and on past many great stopping points. Just when I thought that the preacher had come to a good place to end the sermon, he merely paused and kept going. All too often the sermon continued from fifty minutes to an hour, going beyond numerous good stopping points. After worship the crowds gathered in the cabins, which surrounded the tabernacle, to sit down, visit and eat homemade churned ice cream. The conversation often centered on great sermons and the preachers they remembered from years past. Going to this camp meeting was like going back in history fifty, sixty, seventy or a hundred years. Camp meeting was a strong reminder of an earlier time when the church was the centerpiece of every little country community. Though I was ignorant of the camp meeting culture, I was warmed and inspired by the way the regular attendees welcomed me into their community.

With respect to Smyrna and the camp meeting, as part of my internship I was put in charge of youth camp at the Smyrna Campground. On Sunday before youth camp was to begin, I did not have enough leaders for the week. I had been working very hard to recruit leaders, but they had not been forthcoming. I was a long way behind in securing enough leaders to run the camp. On the morning before the youth camp was to begin, I walked into Carl's office with my head hanging down because I was ashamed that I had not been able to recruit enough leaders. Carl looked at me and smiled. He leaned back in his big desk chair and said, "Well, we will just announce on Sunday that if we don't get enough volunteers to do the work, we will know that we are not to have youth camp this year."

Carl did not worry about anything. He had a deep trust in God. He truly believed that if folks did not voluntarily step up to give leadership to the youth camp or if God did not provide the leadership for the youth camp, we should not have the youth camp. Carl had grown up the grandson of a Primitive Baptist minister. I knew nothing about Primitive Baptists until I learned from Carl that Primitive Baptists believed that everything depended upon God. They believed that God had elected those who would be saved and that he would bring them into the church. So Primitive Baptists did no arm twisting or offer four spiritual laws and there was no strong influence to make Christians out of people. They were committed to the proposition that God would redeem those whom God was pleased to save.

The summer after I had served at Smyrna as an intern, Carl called me. He invited me to preach at the annual camp meeting. This invitation scared me to death. I knew that I could not go on and on in the pulpit like all those camp meeting preachers. To this day I don't know why Carl asked me to preach at the camp meeting. However, I did accept his invitation. On a hot summer day I dragged myself up on the platform to preach as I truly wondered if and how God could use me in this setting. The lady at the piano and the song leaders kept the lively singing going twice as long as regular church service. When I stood up to preach, I deemed that the service should last no longer than one hour, so I cut out half the sermon that I had prepared. I probably preached for ten minutes. It seemed a good thing to me to let people out to get to the ice cream churns before dark. A few of the people complimented my sermon, but for some reason that was the first and last time I was invited to preach at the Smyrna Camp Meeting.

Other significant experiences in my training for ministry revolved around Clinical Pastoral Education, CPE. This pastoral education evolved as a model of experiential education in which ministers visit with patients in the hospital offering them pastoral care. Students serving as chaplains in hospitals or similar institutions provided the setting for experiential learning. I had many life-changing and gut-wrenching encounters as I offered pastoral care to individuals who were struggling with emotional and spiritual issues.

One such incident occurred when I was staying overnight at the hospital and my beeper went off in the middle of the night. I was needed in the Neonatal Intensive Care Unit. When I arrived, I saw a young couple standing by an incubator where their newborn baby lay. The nurse had told me that their baby was dying. The medical staff had given up on any further intervention, believing that nothing would save the child. As I looked at the little baby's lifeless body and observed the expressions on the faces of the bereft young mom and dad, I saw tears flowing down their cheeks. From time to time they held each other, hugged each other tightly and wept from a deep place in their souls. I felt helpless; I had no idea what to say to this young couple. I stood in the room with them speechless. I kept looking for an opportunity to offer some kind of comfort to them. It seemed that I stood there speechless for at least two hours as they grieved the loss of their newborn baby.

The next morning when I met with the couple, the mother said, "Oh, chaplain, thank you so much for being with us last night. The things that you said to us were so very, very helpful." I was conscious that I had said nothing. This experience began to teach me just how important a presence is in the midst of unthinkable grief and loss. In my chaplaincy training I repeatedly encountered situations where people were dying or were in dire straits and felt themselves isolated and alone. Presence, with little or no speech, always made a difference to them.

I spent a year working in an Oncology Unit. On my rounds I met a kind man and his wife. He was dying of cancer. His wife came every day and sat by his side in the hospital room. Little by little, fewer and fewer people opened the door to his room to see this man on his deathbed. In order to be with him, I had to face the reality of my own death. Day by day as I watched him slipping away, I came to love him and his wife. I was amazed at how they were willing to open the most intimate parts of their hearts to me as their chaplain. Together they taught me the tremendous privilege and the inescapable responsibility of carrying the mantle of a minister of Christ. In times like they were facing, many people welcome the opportunity to share their deepest fears and doubts. When people are dealing with death and loss, they are looking for a sympathetic ear. In the dark days at the ending of a life, many friends and even members of the family stay away because they do not know what to say or do. Some of the most intimate and meaningful moments of my life have been spent with the people whom I watched die. In those situations I saw that in difficult and dire circumstances all the pretense which characterizes our culture falls away. And those who are suffering as well as those who care for them are transported into a place of deep connectedness with themselves, with each other and with God. Serving people in the Oncology Unit taught me many lessons about being with people who are dying. For these priceless gifts, I am grateful.

In the hospital I was also privileged to work as a chaplain in the Psychiatric Unit. The staff of that unit was made up of doctors, nurses, therapists, housekeepers, recreation therapists, art therapists and an important band of people from different backgrounds and walks in life. We were black and white; we were Christian and Jewish; we were believers and nonbelievers that focused on the primary goal of caring for people suffering from mental illness. We had a non-structured gathering of everyone who worked on the unit once a week. This group was facilitated by a pastoral counselor whose name was Walter Smith. During my time in the unit, I don't believe I ever heard Walter Smith utter a single word. He simply came into the room, sat down in the midst of this group and looked around at each of us. There was something about his presence that welcomed our speech. He demonstrated to me the power of nonverbal communication. Walter was clearly present to himself and to us and in love he communicated without words. Just his presence invited us to speak whatever was necessary. One of the things that made this a powerful experience was the absence of a hierarchy. Both the psychiatrists and the housekeepers and everyone else in that room were on a par with each other. Often men and women from housekeeping had deeper insights into the patients than the psychiatrists and the chaplains and doctors.

While working in this unit, a memorable experience came to me through a patient who was profoundly depressed. No one could get this patient to come out of her room. Efforts to get her to speak also failed. When they went into her room trying to engage her, she completely ignored them. Then one of the therapists on the unit who was daringly open to taking risks went into her room one day. He tried to engage her as all the other workers had, and she ignored him too. The orderly had just brought her lunch into the room on a tray. The audacious counselor walked over, picked up a roll from the tray and threw it at her; he hit her right in the face. In that moment she picked up food from the tray and threw it back at him. Before long they were in a food fight right there in her room. This unexpected action on the therapist's part created a situation in which she could no longer resist expressing her anger and rage. This incident taught me that redemption occurs in multiple ways and that new experiences often grow out of taking risks. This kind of change does not come from painting by the numbers, but it does come from being present to people and taking risks to create a relationship. Sometimes you don't know what you're doing, but you take risks and deal with the results.

I learned from a number of supervisors and teachers through those years of chaplaincy at Georgia Baptist Medical Center. Those things that I learned in the units and in meeting with therapists and the other staff members truly shaped and influenced my way of counseling. Among those mentors and teachers were Dr. Frank Weathersby and Rev. Don Caviness. Both of these men were wonderful, wild and daring teachers of pastoral care and counseling. Frank had red hair and wore cowboy boots. He did not pay much attention to the editing function of consciousness; whatever he thought, he said and said it clearly and forcefully.

There were other significant persons involved in my training at Georgia Baptist Medical Center who were clearly psychoanalytic. I sometimes thought that the supervisors were more Freudian than Freud. Part of my training was having weekly psychoanalysis with a psychiatrist, Dr. Bill Rottersman. Dr. Rottersman had been a teaching analyst at Menninger Clinic in Topeka, Kansas.

I found psychoanalysis to be a very interesting and revealing process. Each week I went into Dr. Rottersman's office. I entered, lay down on his couch and Dr. Rottersman took his seat in a chair behind me so that he could hear me but we could not look each other in the eye. Week after week, I did most of the talking as Dr. Rottersman silently sat behind me. In one session I noticed that I always talked about the same thing. I said to Dr. Rottersman, "I think I always talk about the same thing when I come to visit with you." His response was a very loud humming sound with no words; then he went silent. He waited for me to continue to speak. It dawned on me that in my analysis I was developing a deeper insight into myself by hearing myself speak.

On another occasion my relation to the analyst got clearer. I was lying on the couch going on and on and suddenly I heard this loud snoring coming from the chair behind me. I said, "Dr. Rottersman, are you there? Are you listening?"

In a very calm voice he said, "Yes. Go ahead, I'm listening."

I began to wonder if I was paying all this money and exerting this energy to simply listen to myself. I began to realize that it didn't really matter what Dr. Rottersman thought. What mattered was my getting clear on who I am and what I think. It amazes me what lengths I had to go to for this basic truth to emerge. Those years with Dr. Rottersman were worth my investment of time and money simply to get this one profound insight.

The insights that I received in clinical training and psychoanalysis gave rise to a greater thirst in me to learn. I became interested in different forms of therapy, different philosophies of change and different effective interventions in troubled lives. After serving in the church for four years, I returned to Georgia Baptist Medical Center to do a three-year residency in pastoral counseling. Leigh Conver, a wonderful teacher, was heading up the training program. Lee had been a student of Dr. Wayne Oates at Southern Baptist Theological Seminary in Louisville, Kentucky. Lee had been recently hired to be in charge of training counselors at Georgia Baptist Medical Center. He was not only certified as a pastoral counselor but was also certified in marriage and family therapy. Marriage and family therapy explores entire family systems and community systems to discover how they act and react and how they change. Psychoanalysis focuses on the individual and the individual psyche and how individuals change in reaction to internal conflicts. Looking at a larger system like that in families, churches and other organizations was exciting to me. This broadened the perspective from limiting the work with individuals only and how individuals change to viewing the whole structure of relationships in family, community and church to see how each acts and reacts to specific issues. Lee helped me begin to see how families operate as a unit. In families, children are unconsciously carrying out missions that have been assigned them by mothers and fathers and grandparents. He helped me to see patterns that are passed down from generation to generation in institutions and in families. This new perspective was enlightening and liberating to me.

Family systems helped me begin to understand my own childhood. I began to see that the conflict between my mother and father involved me. I began to understand how my mother embraced me and my father rejected me, and this behavior was about them and not about me. I saw that my father's family didn't understand my mother and her family. It became clearer to me how my mother's family viewed her as having married beneath herself. Nonverbally they were rejecting the attempts of my father to move closer to them. These energies flowing within my own family had shaped me and put me in a position where I didn't make constructive choices about my future, only decisions that helped me survive the turmoil and the conflict that was a part of my birth family.

In the family systems, it mattered that my mother had come out of a Roman Catholic background, which from the time of the Reformation understood itself as the only true church. My father, who was a Presbyterian, was part the group who were excommunicated from the church. I saw how these patterns and this history passed down from generation to generation between Catholics and Protestants long after the original battle was forgotten. My parents, like so many others, had been innocently impacted and pulled into a battle that went back for generations. And in the community where I was reared, the economy depended on the textile industry. In that community there was a static society in which the white owners and managers of the mills were on top, the mill workers were in the middle, and the blacks were on the bottom of the economic hierarchy, unable to move up in the system.

This system had played down through generations beginning in our mother country, England, where royalty sat at the top of the heap and ordinary individuals were ostracized if they tried to cross the class boundaries. In the south we had another struggle between middle-class and upper-class and along with that issue we had the memory of slavery. I began to understand that I was born and reared in a system where everyone knew his or her place. People did not cross the boundaries of race, culture or religion. This cultural conflict was very clear in York, South Carolina. Those who were Catholics, Episcopalians, Baptists, Presbyterians or Methodists were a little suspicious of each other's beliefs and practices. They certainly did not socialize with each other.

These relationships in many ways were dictated by race, religion, class and social standing. The insecurities in these communities played out in a "me and mine" attitude versus "you and yours."

CHAPTER EIGHT

Serving Presbyterian Churches

*

AFTER I COMPLETED SEMINARY and two years of clinical training, I was not sure where I would go next. One afternoon I stopped at a filling station down the street from the seminary and there I encountered Davison Philips. At the time he was the president of Columbia Seminary. Actually, he had served as president for the entire time I had been a student. He greeted me with a big smile and then said, "Robby, Frank Harrington is looking for an associate at Peachtree Presbyterian Church. I am going to call Frank and recommend you for that job." I was humbled by the confidence that Davison Philips showed in me. It was hard for me to believe that Davison Philips would recommend me as an associate to the largest Presbyterian Church in the United States. I had come to seminary so late in life that I had the gnawing feeling I would not be a great minister or make an outstanding contribution to the church.

In a few days my phone rang. Calling was Chuck Mann, who was the senior associate at Peachtree Presbyterian Church. Chuck told me that Frank Harrington, the Senior Pastor at Peachtree, wanted to meet with me. The call came in the summer when Frank was at Hilton Head, South Carolina vacationing and preparing sermons for the coming church year. To meet with Frank, Chuck Mann explained to me that he would pick me up and take me to the airport to be flown to Hilton Head.

Billy Merritt, one of the elders at Peachtree, would fly both Jane and me to Hilton Head for the meeting. Wow! Was that a surprise to me! Being flown in a private plane to Hilton Head to interview for a church job. This was my introduction to Frank Harrington and Peachtree. My mother-in-law, when she heard about these plans, gave a prophetic statement: "Robby, I guarantee you that this will be the last time you'll fly in a private airplane to get a preacher's job." How right she was. I haven't been in a private plane for any reason since that day.

After meeting with Frank over a delightful dinner at a classy restaurant at Hilton Head, we flew back to Atlanta. The next day I got a call from the chair of the pulpit nominating committee, and this efficient woman, Betty Eberhardt, asked me to meet her at the Cherokee Country Club for lunch. Jane and I met with Betty and had a delightful meal and a good interview. It was clear to me that this pulpit nominating committee worked differently from many search committees. Frank had obviously informed Betty that I was the candidate that he wanted called to be his associate. And, I was thrilled to get a call to a church in Atlanta. My role at Peachtree Church was to minister to single adults.

When I was called to Peachtree, they had a membership of about five thousand. The church had already begun a Tuesday evening program, "For Singles Only." I was the first minister on the staff to focus exclusively on single adults. Peachtree was located in Buckhead, an upscale community of Atlanta. The area was filled with young adults who worked in businesses and schools throughout Atlanta. With its television ministry and focus on young families and working singles, Peachtree drew a large number of visitors each Sunday. Literally, hundreds of single adults had moved to Atlanta seeking jobs and opportunities. Many single adults came to Peachtree to meet other single adults. With this potential almost any response to this group's needs was a great success. There were so many searching people that no matter what idea I proposed, thirty or forty folks would show up for it.

I quickly learned that in church as in business the importance of location, location, location held very true. All the churches in the Buckhead area -- the Episcopal Cathedral of St. Philip, Wieuca Road Baptist Church, Second Ponce de Leon Baptist Church and Peachtree Road United Methodist Church -- were all large, successful churches. I realized how fortunate I was to have the opportunity to serve in the Peachtree Church. Frank Harrington, the Senior Minister, was a brilliant preacher, pastor and a magnetic personality. He was greatly loved and respected in the community.

Frank Harrington had the same brilliance in the way he connected with all kinds of people from presidents to men who shined his shoes. He went to the hospitals in the area almost every afternoon visiting people who were sick and in need of spiritual comfort. He focused his time and attention on visiting with folks who visited Peachtree Presbyterian Church. Monthly, on Thursday evenings Frank hosted new member dinners at the church. At least one hundred new members attended each month for fellowship and a meal. Each month at these dinners, Frank gave the keynote address. After the dinner and before he spoke, various new members were interviewed. Generally, they were asked why they decided to join Peachtree Presbyterian Church. Over and over the answer came, "I joined to get Frank Harrington out of my living room." Frank had an amazing gift for helping people feel at home and welcomed in the church. I value the many things I learned about connecting with people from him.

While I was on staff at Peachtree, I began to do a great deal of counseling. I had significant training in chaplaincy prior to coming to Peachtree, and I spent many hours in the church being a chaplain to single young adults. At this time I also initiated a Divorce Recovery Program, which became an immense success among those who had suffered the end of their marriage. I trained numerous small group leaders to facilitate groups in this divorce recovery ministry. Almost thirty years later, I continued to meet with the small group leaders in this program. Frank Harrington recognized in me the gifts for pastoral care and counseling. He asked me to develop a new model for a counseling center at Peachtree.

With this task in mind I met with leaders in pastoral counseling in the Atlanta area. These authorities included Dr. John Patton and Dr. Jap Keith. I asked for their assistance in establishing a counseling center at Peachtree. As we explored different models of a counseling ministry, it became clear that John Patton and Jap Keith would do the interviewing and approving of potential counselors for the Peachtree Counseling Center. Handing over the authority to someone outside the Peachtree church obviously made Frank very nervous. In the final analysis he was clearly not willing to have anyone working at Peachtree without his personal approval. The direction in which the planning was going would not get Frank's approval. Hitting this unmovable snag was a major disappointment to me. Not long after this initiative fell apart Frank expressed a willingness to hire an intern to help me with the singles and counseling ministry.

One Saturday morning I was at home with Jane when the phone rang. It was Frank. In his mind every staff member was on call for him and any new idea that he might have. Without hesitation he said, "I want you to come to the church right now; I must talk to you about this intern we are hiring." Frank wanted me to drop everything, get in the car and come to the church at a moment's notice. Putting it mildly, Jane was irate. She had taken all that she could bear of Frank's demand for complete devotion and his thoughtlessness about the personal life of his staff. Frank was a very hard-working, dedicated minister, and he expected each one of his staff members to be available to him at any and every moment.

After several years of work at Peachtree, I was approached by a pulpit nominating committee from Decatur Presbyterian Church. They invited me to come to Decatur as the minister of Pastoral Care and Evangelism. As I interacted with the pulpit nominating committee, it seemed to me that God was offering me a pathway that could bring greater peace to my family, an enlarged ministry and perhaps an opportunity for additional training. I loved my work at Peachtree Presbyterian Church, but my work was becoming more and more difficult for me and my family because of the huge load of work and some of the unrealistic demands being placed on me. I responded to this call from Decatur Presbyterian Church and began my ministry there in 1985.

Private Practice

I served as the minister of pastoral care at Decatur for only two years. My work there was productive, but this was a time of transition in that particular church. One of the memorable events that took place while I was at Decatur has lingered with me – the death of my father.

His death forced me to reflect on the relationship that we had had for forty-four years, which was seriously conflicted. I was born in 1943 while he was away in the Army Air Corps. He came home for a few days at the time of my birth and was in the hospital when the minister preformed my baptism. While my father was away I bonded with my mother, grandmother and sisters, and this tended to distance me further from my father. When he came home from the war, I had the perception that my mother preferred me over him. I was often the object of fights and disagreements that went on between them.

When he attacked me with his rage, my mother came to my defense. As I look back, it seems that I represented the disconnect between my mother's family of origin and my father's family. My father must have had deep wounds during his childhood that created his overly negative reactions to me. In later years when I was studying to become a therapist, I attempted to speak with him about his childhood, but he never shared himself with me. My experience with him and my seeking to understand him and the conflict between us has greatly influenced my work as a therapist.

I think that my empathy for people comes from the little boy in me who was abused and gives me an understanding of the human condition. One night I had a dream. In the dream my father and I were riding in his new, expensive car. He was well dressed with gold cuff links and a white handkerchief in his suit jacket. As we drove along, I finally was able to engage him about some of the painful aspects of his childhood. I wept as I shared with him my understanding of what it must have been like for him to be locked up by his parents in a small, dark closet. I had compassion for the little boy who stuttered so badly and had to repeat himself several times to be understood. I wondered what it must have been like to have all four of his siblings graduate from fine colleges when he barely made it through high school.

Sometime later after my father's death, I had another dream in which I saw my father passing through the fires of hell. The fires burned off all of his fears, defenses and insecurities. As the fires burned, his true and undefended self was increasingly revealed more clearly. Those redemptive, purifying flames liberated him to be who he was at his core. He was a good man who meant no harm. He, like so many of us, did the best that he could with his life. As I reflect on this powerful dream I am reminded of the many ways that difficulty and hardship have been redemptive in my own life. The Serenity Prayer says it well:

"God grant me the serenity to accept the things
I cannot change; the courage to change the things
I can; and wisdom to know the difference.
Living one day at a time; enjoying one moment at a
time; accepting hardships as the pathway to peace;
taking, as He did, this sinful world as it is, not
as I would have it; trusting that He will make all
things right if I surrender to His Will; that I may be
reasonably happy in this life and supremely happy
with Him forever in the next.
Amen.

These dreams and this prayer have helped me lay to rest my painful memories of my relationship with my father.

After I left Decatur Presbyterian Church to go into private practice as a pastoral counselor, I spent the years from 1987 until 2003 in an office outside of a church where I saw numerous patients daily. During those years I also served on the Presbytery Committee on the Ministry. At that time Bill Adams was our Presbytery Executive. Bill utilized me as a consultant to troubled churches and churches that were going through transition. I worked with numerous churches during those years. I also led small consultation groups with Presbyterian ministers. In addition to my consultation work with the Presbytery, I served as a consultant to the adult rehabilitation centers of the Salvation Army. I traveled around the southern territory of the Salvation Army teaching leaders in the adult rehabilitation centers how to set up and run Celebrate Recovery Programs in their centers. I learned a great deal from my work with the Salvation Army. It is a powerful experience to see men move from addiction and crime in the streets into recovery and new life in Christ. An experience in Miami illustrates the reason for my excitement in working with these men in recovery. While I was working with the leaders, we went out to lunch in the Salvation Army van with a number of men who were residents in the adult rehabilitation center.

On the way to lunch we passed by a particular street corner and the man sitting next to me tapped me on the shoulder and said, "Do you see that corner over there?

I said, "Yes, I see it."

He said, "I was standing right there when I was shot before I went to prison. This is where I hung out and dealt drugs. There was a time when I knew everybody who lived in this neighborhood. They were all afraid of me and walked away when they saw me coming. It was not until I was arrested and spent time in prison that my life turned around. I am so grateful for the work of the Salvation Army and for Celebrate Recovery. Jesus Christ has given me a new lease on life."

Shallowford Presbyterian Church

Being associated with the Shallowford Presbyterian Church has been one of the most delightful experiences of my entire ministry. In 2003 Bill Carr, my friend who was serving at Shallowford as a parish associate, was called into the reserves to go to Kuwait. Bill recommended me to Gray Norsworthy, Shallowford's senior pastor, as someone to fill in for him while he spent a year on active duty. Gray called me, we met for lunch and after a long conversation about Shallowford, he asked me to work with him. Afterward I met with the personnel committee, and they offered me a position for one year until Bill returned from active duty. I began my service at Shallowford in February 2003. Truly, Shallowford is a wonderful congregation of many good and committed people. They welcomed me with open arms to this temporary position while Bill Carr served in Kuwait. After Bill spent a year on active duty with the reserves, he decided to continue his active duty with the military. Bill remained on active duty until he retired. When it was clear that Bill would not be returning to Shallowford, I was offered the opportunity to remain at Shallowford, and it has been a great blessing in my life to serve at Shallowford Presbyterian Church.

My role was to be a parish associate for pastoral care and counseling. My responsibilities included visiting in hospitals and nursing homes, offering individual counseling to people, and facilitating an Alzheimer's support group, which had been formed about four years earlier to support those individuals who were caring for someone with dementia.

In addition, I offered pastoral care and counseling to individuals facing challenging life experiences. An opportunity for this help came one morning when Ona Stanley called my office. Ona was a member of our Alzheimer's group. Ona worked out of her home as a seamstress

81

since most of her time was devoted to taking care of her mother, who had Alzheimer's. During the period of caring for her mother, she discovered that she, herself, had cancer. Ona was a beautifully transparent, loving woman who was open to sharing her life experiences with others. One day as she and I spoke together, I asked her about making a video of her experience of facing her own death. I explained that I thought her story could be useful in training other caregivers. I wanted to explore with her the diagnosis of her cancer, the decisions she had made and how she dealt with the fact that she knew she was dying. Ona was very open to sharing this experience through a recording.

I asked one of our members who is in the television recording industry if he would be willing to help me with this project. Coincidentally, I learned that Mike Chase, the cameraman, had also seen his mother through a bout with cancer. This was no new experience for him. On the day we had set to interview Ona, I met Mike at her house. We entered Ona's living room and sat down on the sofa. When she got comfortable and was ready, I began to ask her questions. When I asked her about her experience in getting the diagnosis, she explained the long and painful process in which the first physician had misdiagnosed her. That misdiagnosis resulted in a significant loss of time in properly treating the cancer. As the cancer progressed and she was getting worse by the day, she finally reached out to another doctor. He immediately diagnosed her issue properly and started her on chemotherapy.

I asked Ona what had been the most helpful encounters that she had had with people after her diagnosis. I wanted to know how Ona had felt cared for by those around her. She said that when people were simply present and listened to her, she felt the deepest connection and most care. She said it was a rare gift when people would simply listen and allow her to express the pain, the disappointment, the fear and other difficult emotions that she experienced while knowing that her days were limited. She also explained the kinds of questions and encounters that were least helpful to her. Folks who said that they knew "things were going to be better" or there was "hope for a miracle if she only trusted God" did her no good. Comments that minimized her condition and the experience that she was having pushed her feelings aside and made her feel discounted. Ona helped me to understand how important it is for those offering pastoral care to manage their own fears and anxieties. What the sufferer needs is for caregivers to simply listen to the pain and fear that's being expressed.

The Alzheimer's group at Shallowford has offered rich support to numerous caregivers. Ted Bayley in particular was greatly loved by Shallowford Church; he was a committed man who served others all of his life. Ted had several altruistic vocations; he served as a director for the Boy Scouts of America, giving himself unselfishly for the well-being of young boys. After serving in that capacity he took a Master's in Business Administration and later became the Officer of Development for St. Joseph's Hospital.

In addition to his job with St. Joseph's, he served on the committee charged with the task of calling a new associate presbyter to the Presbytery of Greater Atlanta. Ted chaired that committee and did a stellar job of lining up and interviewing candidates and leading the committee in making their selection. The committee called Ruth Hicks, who did a magnificent job; Ted had an important part in finding and getting Ruth to serve in our Presbytery.

It came as quite a shock to many of us when Ted began to show symptoms of memory loss and difficulty with directions. When he was diagnosed with Alzheimer's, he volunteered to become part of an experimental group to test medications for Alzheimer sufferers. He looked upon his participation in this group as a way that he might help others; this attitude of self-giving gave him a reason for living day by day.

Each week he came to our Thursday morning men's prayer breakfast. Group members took turns cooking the food, and after a sumptuous breakfast every man around the table said a prayer. Ted's prayers always expressed a deep concern for others and a desire to serve the community more faithfully. When his Alzheimer's got to an advanced stage and he could not carry on a conversation, he could still pray intelligible prayers. Slowly, bit by bit Ted began to lose the sharpness of his mind. Week after week we could see the degeneration of his thought processes. For weeks even as Ted was barely able to speak, he put on his Marine hat and walked from his house to the church to attend the breakfast meeting. What a painful process it was to see Ted leave us as he did.

I was moved by the way Ellen, Ted's wife, cared for him at home for several years. When Ted's disease got the best of him, Ellen finally had to put him in Fountainview Nursing Home where he could receive care twenty-four hours a day. Ellen and their daughter Karen stayed by his side, supporting him, loving him, caring for him in the ways that he had cared for them. Ellen began to attend our Alzheimer's support group where people are encouraged to simply tell their stories. We rule out giving advice; we discourage interrupting people as they speak; and we ask the group to keep confidences so that people feel free to express thoughts and feelings, whatever they may be.

In situations like Ted Bayley's, family members don't know whether to pray for their loved one to live, or to give them up because their loved one looks the same but is no longer responsive. Ellen has been deeply appreciative of the group experience. The group has been a place where she could share her confusion and loss as the light was going out in Ted little by little. She also was able to hear the stories of others who had the same questions she had. Being in a group enables people to feel support and not be so alone fighting their battle. When caring people seek to make it on their own, they begin to feel that no one else understands what they are going through. Hearing others tell their stories provides common ground. Some people have described the Alzheimer's disease as the long, long goodbye. How can one go on believing day after day, when the loved one keeps going downhill? The group is a place in which people can put their arms, hearts and spirits around each other and make the journey together.

New Pastor

After some years the senior minister at Shallowford, Gray Norsworthy, got a call to another church. His departure gave rise to the necessity of an interim head of staff for six months while the search committee looked for a full-time interim. During this period I served as the interim head of staff. Then, Bruce Meyers was hired as the interim for a year and a half. The Pastor Nominating Committee at Shallowford was committed to spending as long as it took to find the right new minister. After many hours of reading Personal Information Forms and an equal number of hours interviewing prospects, the committee found a likely candidate in a young man who was serving nearby at the

Morningside Presbyterian Church. After the members of the search committee heard him preach and thoroughly interviewed him, they took the next step and invited him to meet with the staff of our church.

One evening the staff went to the home of Bridges and Betsy Smith to meet the prospective pastor. We interviewed each other for about an hour. After getting to know Chris, we were all deeply impressed with his gifts and with him as a person. He also demonstrated a profound understanding of the church. After meeting and talking with him, I was convinced that Chris Henry was the right person for Shallowford, if God allowed us to get him.

By this time the committee had become convinced that this was the right man for the church, and they called Christopher Andrew Henry to be the Senior Minister and Head of Staff; at the time he was only twenty-eight years of age. In just a few weeks Chris said "yes" to the call of God. Many of us believe in God's Providence and that it was God's Providence that brought this young man to us. He is quite unusual. Savvy beyond his years, he is masterful in all the roles of a pastor; he is an effective preacher, teacher, counselor, pastoral caregiver and administrator. How could we ask for more? When he came to be our senior pastor, I not only was grateful for the choice of the search committee, I believed that his leadership would make my own ministry more effective. My hopes have not been disappointed.

When Chris arrived, I felt called to do everything I could to help him get connected with the whole congregation. As it turned out, this man did not need much help from me. Through his eyes we have seen a new vision and have found strength to carry it out. We have a newly renovated chapel and youth space. We have taken in a significant number of new members. We have formed new Sunday school classes and small groups. We have a new mission statement that inspires us all. Our mission is to invite all people to a faithful way of life in community and in Christ. And, this is just the beginning.

Chapter Nine

Reflections on Family and Life Together

_____

✳

In the fall of 1960 I returned home from Christ School in Arden, North Carolina and attended Greenville High School. Each morning that fall I picked up my friend Kirby Hammond at his house and gave him a ride to school. Through him I met the young girl who would eventually become my wife, Jane Hammond, Kirby's little sister. When I was a junior at Greenville High, she was in the ninth grade. Often when I was visiting Kirby, I had long talks with Jane and her mom. This usually occurred when I dropped Kirby off from school. Jane and I, however, never dated in high school.

The summer that Jane made her debut I was her escort to the ball. During the hot, sweaty days of summer, I loaded trucks during the day and in the evenings I went to fancy parties. All these parties led to a large debutante ball at which young women escorted by young men were presented to the local society. .

The presentation of the eligible young ladies took place at the Assembly. The Assembly was a debutante club formed primarily to introduce young women to society. It was their coming out party. The Assembly is part of a very, very old tradition.

When I was asked to escort Jane, I knew that the Assembly was a white tie affair with both young and old men wearing tails and little white bow ties. All the women dressed in evening gowns. At this ball the cocktails flowed freely. I don't recall all the intricacies of the ball, but I do remember drinking a lot of liquor.

When the young women were about to be presented, we formed a long line and the spotlight focused on each couple individually as we marched to the music of Lester Lanin and his band. I recall standing in line and waiting until I heard the announcer say over the loudspeaker, "Miss Jane Gower Hammond is presented by her grandmother and escorted by Mr. Robert Lindsay Carroll, Jr." At that electric moment, Jane and I walked calmly down a long ramp nodding to the crowd of adoring observers on either side of the ballroom. I felt like a dashing young prince, yet truthfully I was anything but that.

Two years after this debutante ball, Jane transferred from Winthrop College to the University of South Carolina. When she showed up at the university, I met her and helped her find her way through the complicated process of class registration. After she came to the university, Jane and I began an uninterrupted relationship. We started dating, and she was my chosen date for all the fraternity parties. I must confess that those years at the University of South Carolina were years of great merriment and frivolity. Jane and I attended numerous parties, made trips to the beach, excursions to the mountains and filled our college days with a full social life and that competed with a lesser devotion to my diligent study; it was indeed a merry time. Even though she was a few years younger than I, Jane graduated from college a year before me. At the time of her graduation we were near a decision to get married and build a life together.

Before I could ask her to marry me, I thought that I should buy a ring to offer her when I proposed. My father had a good friend who had a jewelry store in Greenville, a Mr. Locker. One day I went down to his store and told Mr. Locker that I wanted the biggest, clearest, brightest, cheapest diamond he had. All my life I had looked for a deal in everything, and buying this ring was no exception. He showed me a diamond that must have been a caret and a half; I purchased it and he placed it in a beautiful setting. That very evening I took that ring over to Jane's house to propose. Sitting on her mother's red sofa in their living room, I reached into my pocket, pulled out the box containing the ring and presented it to Jane with the words, "Will you marry me?"

She immediately said, "Yes." That was an unforgettable moment in both our lives. From that night we began making plans for our wedding. Since I lacked another year to graduate from college, Jane's mother pleaded with us to wait until I finished college to get married. We, of course, were younger and wiser than she, so we made plans to have the wedding as soon as possible.

After that night of proposal and engagement, Jane began showing her diamond to her friends and their families. One day Jane pointed out to me that deep inside the diamond there was a big black spot. Soon we were able to see only that black carbon spot when we looked at the biggest, brightest and cheapest diamond that I could buy. Purchasing this cheap diamond came back to haunt me. Needless to say, we took the diamond back to Mr. Locker and traded it in on a pure diamond with no spot.

My foolish, fiscal conservatism showed itself in another way. In the Greenville tradition, a groom always gave a wedding present to his bride. I thought long and hard about what gift I could give Jane. Finally, I came up with the perfect gift, an Electrolux vacuum cleaner. I figured that this gift would serve two purposes: a groom's gift and a vacuum cleaner for the new home that we would be buying anyway. When I was making these plans, with tongue in cheek I thought: "Something warm and personal like a vacuum cleaner will certainly win high praise from Jane." To my utter surprise no one was impressed with my gift, especially Jane. I am grateful that in spite of my social impairment, Jane loves and cares for me anyway. She accepts me just as I am, a gift few would offer me.

On February 3, 1968 at a big, formal wedding at First Presbyterian Church in Greenville, Dr. Neuman Faulkner, who had been Jane's pastor for many years, married us. We had eight groomsmen and eight bridesmaids for this flamboyant affair. We invited five hundred friends and family members to attend. After the wedding we had an impressive reception at the Poinsett Club, which brought together our sources of support for Jane's and my marriage. I have affectionate memories of that day which included welcoming friends, saying our vows, exchanging rites and getting a big kiss in the presence of all who gathered. After the wedding we had a brief honeymoon in Boone, North Carolina.

Immediately after the short honeymoon we returned to Columbia to continue my classes at the University of South Carolina. Jane joined me because she was teaching at the A. C. Flora High School in Columbia. I look back on those early days of marriage with some regret because I was wholly unconscious of what it meant to be a husband and to share equally in a marriage. Jane moved into the apartment where I had been living before we were married. In those early days of marriage, I expected her to join ME in MY life. I had no appreciation of the notion of building a life together. For example, I had money through an inheritance and Jane was a hard-working schoolteacher, and I expected her to pay her share of our living expenses. When I review those days, I am ashamed and disappointed with my selfishness. I would describe myself as a male chauvinist who was drinking far too much. I didn't realize how much I had to learn about creating a loving and caring relationship. Thank God that Jane stayed with me all those years before I learned how to have a loving relationship.

My flagrant disrespect for her can be clearly seen when we were getting the apartment ready for her to move in. I had some friends over who were helping us clean up the apartment and in the midst of this project I was ordering Jane around, telling her what to do. I gave her all the difficult tasks while my friends and I were drinking beer, telling jokes and generally wasting time. Suddenly, from across the room Jane hurled a sponge at me and it hit me on the side of my head, giving me a taste of her anger and rage. Perhaps it took this outburst for me to recognize what she was feeling. Today, I am grateful for this incident that confronted me with my self-centeredness. Jane has always been quick to let me know when I treat her with disrespect, and she is also quick to forgive and accept me.

A year after our marriage, I got my degree in Business Administration. Upon graduation I did not have a clue about what to do next. As I searched for a direction in my life, I decided to enroll in law school. I took the examination and was accepted into the University of South Carolina School of Law where I began classes in the fall of 1969. I seemed to have no difficulty understanding the material my professors assigned. I found the study of contracts, torts and case law very interesting and challenging. However, after two months I became depressed when I began to feel that the practice of law was not my calling, meaning I still had no idea what to do with my life.

In law school we did case studies to learn the law and the principles behind the law. One particular case that we studied involved a family who had a swimming pool in their backyard. They had built a high fence around the swimming pool and even covered the pool with a canvas to keep children out of it. On one occasion the family went out of town. While they were away, some children crawled over the fence and cut a hole in the top of the canvas and jumped into the pool. One of the children got trapped under the canvas cover and drowned. I was astounded at the outcome of that case. The family that owned the pool was found liable for the death of the child because they had an "attractive nuisance" in their backyard. How insane is that? Repeatedly, I heard students say, "You have to love the law." I certainly did not love the law because in so many cases the law seemed to promote anything but justice.

Another case involved the crash of an airliner. The manufacturer of the sophisticated instruments in the airplane was found to be negligent and thus responsible for the people who lost their lives in the crash. The court ruled that the company was negligent and thus liable. The company was found liable because it had the deepest pockets of anyone involved with the crash. I didn't love the law and my depression in part sprang from my disappointment with the law, but it mostly stemmed from my not knowing what to do with my life. I dropped out of law school and began driving a taxi cab in Columbia.

During that year I was contacted by Lib Thomas of Thomas Travel Service, Inc. She had grown up in Greenville where our families knew each other, and their family had moved to Griffin, Georgia. Thomas Travel Service, Inc. needed someone to escort a college tour to Europe, which was to take place in the summer. She offered Jane and me the opportunity to serve as escorts for this European tour. This offer seemed to us a great opportunity, and we jumped at the chance. The tour began in London, crossed the English Channel to the continent and covered Paris, Rome and several other major cities in Europe. After we returned, the Thomas Travel Service offered me an opportunity to open an office for them in Athens, home of the University of Georgia. We moved to Athens and opened the office along with Lib Thomas's daughter. After working in the travel business for a couple of years, I was offered a more challenging opportunity to return to Greenville and work in a building supply company owned by a family friend.

The Wherry family owned the Dealer Supply Lumber Company. Knox Wherry was a close childhood friend of mine and his father, Jack, was a good friend of my father. They invited me to work for them and learn the business with the promise that one day Knox and I would run the company together. My training at Dealer Supply Lumber Company was based on a tested model of having prospective managers work their way up in the company by operating every aspect of the business. Learning how a business really works on a day-to-day basis was a revelation to me. I learned about different kinds of building materials and, perhaps more significantly, I also learned what it means to be a blue-collar worker.

I spent most of my seven years from 1971 to 1978 at Dealer Supply loading trucks and working on production. I treasure what many of the wise blue-collar workers taught me about the company and about myself. Grady Brooks, an African-American man, was at least twenty years older than I. Grady had the ability to repair every type of door or window known to man. He was also an accomplished forklift driver. When a carload of molding, doors and window parts arrived from across the country, we unloaded them and stacked them in the assigned bins.

These boxcar loads of building materials were parked on a railing site behind the warehouse. Before we could unload these boxcars, big, heavy, steel doors that sealed the boxcars had to be opened to get access to the shipment. Often the doors were bent and rusted and difficult to open. Once when Grady was on the forklift, he backed it up and when he went forward to push the door open, the forklift bent the side of the door. I said to Grady, "You are going to bend that door and we will never get it closed." Grady turned his head and looked at me and said, "Robby, right now I'm working on getting this door open and when we get that boxcar unloaded, we'll work at getting this door closed." What wisdom! Through Grady I learned a good deal about doing what you're doing when you are doing it!

Larry Dean Case also taught me the building trade when I was working at Dealer Supply. Larry grew up on a farm outside of Greenville; he was filled with the wisdom that comes from living close to the earth. One day when I felt overloaded with work, I ran through the warehouse looking for Larry. When I found him, I said, "Larry, we are flooded with trucks to load and if you will help stack that new stock, you will really save me a mountain of time." Larry paused and looked at me and said, "Robby, what are you going to do with that time?" I became silent. This was a question I've asked myself over and over, "What are you going to do with that time you saved?"

In the summer of 1973 Jane and I were blessed with our first child. It was a long and difficult birth. Jane was in labor for thirty-six hours. Finally, the doctor made the decision to deliver the baby by C-section. When we returned home with our new baby, we faced other problems. Jane had undergone surgery as well as having endured a long and tiring time of labor. Our little girl, Jane Gower, was a colicky baby. We were inexperienced and frightened parents. The first day when we returned from the hospital, I found myself wondering if I was up to the task of being a dad. Thank God my mother had hired a nursemaid to stay with us for two weeks. She helped us get settled with our new baby and learn how to feed her, change her diapers and care for her.

The early years of Jane Gower's life were difficult for us. Jane's friends gave her one piece of advice; the pediatrician gave her another piece of advice; my family added yet another piece of advice, and this was topped off with her mother's direction. By the grace of God we survived those years of knowing nothing about how to be parents. Our knowledge grew from on the job training.

When Jane Gower was born, I was working long hours every day. By this time at Dealer Supply, I was in charge of shipping and receiving in the warehouse. I arrived at the company by 6:00 a.m. every morning to line up the day's projects before the workers arrived. I often remained at work until 7:00 or 8:00 p.m. because every truck had to be loaded for an early departure. During those years I left home before my little girl got up and came home after she had gone to bed. Like the earlier years of our marriage, I was not very available to Jane and my daughter.

Frustrated by work and my inability to organize my time, I began to drink more heavily. After work I often went to a local watering hole with the guys to have a few beers before heading home. Sometimes on Saturday I drank a whole case of beer. I was able to function well at work, but my drinking began to take a toll on my relationship with Jane and my emotional availability to her. Day after day my alcoholism more and more became a problem affecting everything in my life, particularly my family.

In the summer of 1976 Jane gave birth to our son, Robert Lindsay Carroll, III.   Robert was a cute little boy, full of life; he was both warm and loving. He engaged with us and with his surroundings in a beautiful way. Our good years came before he began kindergarten. After he began kindergarten at the Decatur Presbyterian Church, it soon became evident that he could not keep up with the other children. When we visited with his teacher, she told us that Robert was not engaging the material; rather, he sat with her at the back of the room while the other children were learning to read and count. From the very beginning Robert showed signs of having a severe learning disability. When it came time for Robert to enter the first grade, we had him tested for Special Education classes. He was offered a Diagnostic Position in a DeKalb County school, which would be an opportunity to deal more effectively with his disability. I didn't know what "Diagnostic Position" meant or how it worked. I feared that the teachers would not recognize that he had severe learning issues. So we decided to send him to a private school.

Jane and I continued to search for help for Robert. We found a private school, an Atlanta school that focused on children with specific learning disabilities. We entered Robert in classes with the staff's promise that they taught children in the way that they were best able to learn. They employed visual, auditory and kinesthetic experiences that fit each child's needs. We were greatly disappointed when we learned that in reality their methods revolved around repetition, a practice that did not interest or enable Robert at all. In those years Robert's self-esteem continued to plummet. Robert was unable to be successful either in learning or in social adaptation. His plight reminded me of a young boy for whom the carrot was too high and the whip was too harsh. When the school did not aid Robert's development, we sent him to Gables Academy for a couple of years. This academy in Atlanta was advertised as a small private school for children who had learning and personality problems.

In an effort to help him keep up with his peers, Jane and I continued to investigate ways to help Robert learn and grow. Jane stumbled onto a Special Education professional who would tutor Robert individually.

From our home it was several miles to Susan Dehoff's office where she worked with Robert. On the way to her office Robert yelled, screamed and beat on the car door because to him the search for learning felt like punishment. He would much rather have gone outside to play every day than go to classes of any kind. On the days that we did not take Robert to Susan for tutoring, we all saw a child psychiatrist at Emory. The visits with this psychiatrist were also painful and difficult for us as well as Robert. From where I view the experience today, those visits were even counterproductive. Psychiatry often makes problems out of things that are not problems. Psychiatry focuses on pathology, which explores what is wrong with an individual. I believe that we needed more focus on what was right with the person. Certainly, a setting that put all the emphasis on academic achievement was not the right place for Robert. Maybe he could have flourished in the unfolding of his life if he had grown up on a farm; if he had spent his time in manual labor and growing vegetables and flowers, life might have been different. Robert was good with his hands and a very hard worker. Throughout those early developmental years all of the emphasis in Robert's life revolved around tasks that he simply could not do.

I wonder if we are a culture that worships at the feet of academia. If this suggestion is a fact, what a disservice to a significant portion of our population. I know of no place today for a little boy with Roberts's deficiencies and personality type. When I reflect on these years and the different schools that we tested, I realize that I grew up in an era when Special Education did not exist. Special Education, working with children who had particular needs, was seen as an advance in our culture. Special Education also has its pronounced downside: when all the maladjusted children are lumped together, where are their positive role models? The children who could possibly model a better way of handling conflicts are absent.

Another influence in Robert's life was his sister, Jane Gower. Being a different personality, she seemed to do well in almost everything she undertook. She went to public schools and did well in her studies. Friendships with other kids in the neighborhood seemed to come naturally to her. In sports, swimming for example, she competed on the team. Robert received a great deal of attention from her; she was close to him and untiringly helpful to her little brother.

After attending both Agnes Scott College and the University of Georgia and working in Atlanta for several years, Jane Gower married Mark Turner. For me the highlight of their marriage came with the births of their daughter Mary Elizabeth and their son Mark, our first grandchildren.

Jane Gower is in many ways like me. She is full of energy, always exploring and wrestling with all the obstacles that life brings. What manifested as a strong will when she was a little girl has blossomed into a "can do," energetic, productive woman. Though our children were challenges to us young, inexperienced parents, I thank God every day for both of them and the way they have enriched our lives.

Parenting has been a blessing and has pushed me to grow up. Learning to communicate with our children is different from any other relationship in life. Becoming a good parent requires persistent effort; we have gone and we will continue to go to great lengths to nurture and empower them for life. I might also add that struggling through my own family problems has grounded and given focus to the counseling I offer to other parents.

Chapter Ten

Streams of Influence

�֍

How do my previous experiences affect my life and the work that I do? How can I discover the lenses through which I see the world or the filters through which I listen to the problems and conflicts of others? I plan to use the reflections that I now set forth to examine how all these streams of influence have coalesced into a consortium of perception, knowledge and behavior peculiar to me. So for my own benefit and also that of the people with whom I have counseled, I continue to ask myself three questions: What are the experiences that I have had in therapy and personal growth? What did these experiences do in my own life? And, how do they inform my work with other people?

Psychoanalytic Studies

My original clinical training in Pastoral Care and Counseling was at Georgia Baptist Medical Center where I did an internship and residency. The primary theoretical framework for the training was psychoanalytic. We studied the work and contributions of Sigmund Freud. In addition to the study of Freud's work we were all in analysis with psychoanalysts. Other training centers focused on a more eclectic approach studying many psychological theorists. The perspective of the training team at Georgia Baptist Center for Pastoral Care and Counseling required all interns to gain an in-depth understanding of Freudian Analysis.

Without going into great detail about this theory the major perspective is that personality and patterns of behavior, thought and emotions are formed in the first five years of life. This being the case, problems in the here and now have their basis in mostly unconscious patterns, which were established very early in life as a way of adapting to the context that the individual was born into. These patterns continue to play out throughout our life until we gain insight into where they originated. This insight is seen as the intervention that frees a person to adapt to the current context.

From this deterministic perspective early patterns of adaptation continue throughout life in spite of its changing context. With this general theory as a guide in therapy we habitually say, "Tell me about your Mama and them."

Neuro-Linguistic Programing

Neuro-Linguistic Programming, or NLP as it is called, is a field of therapy and ways of change that emerged from the work of Milton Erickson, Fritz Perls and Virginia Satir. It is a discerning approach that pays close attention to the possibilities for change in others through modeling behavior as well as through defining in sensory terms desired outcomes in life. This perspective highlights the ways in which our beliefs and presuppositions in life affect the results that we achieve. NLP suggests a number of proposals that, if adopted, can lead to desirable results and empower people to achieve higher levels of self-actualization.

These principles are not claimed to be universally true. You do not have to believe that they are true. These presuppositions are presupposed to be true and acted on as if they are true. A person who practices them discovers that they are true by the results that occur. If the results are desirable, they continue to act as if they are true. They form a set of ethical principles for life which I will set forth.

1. People respond to their experience, not to reality itself. Our senses, beliefs and past experiences give us a map of the world from which we operate. A map can never be exactly accurate, but some maps are better than others for finding one's way. When maps are faulty and do not show the dangers, travelers are liable to run aground. NLP is the art of changing these

97

maps, to give greater freedom of action.

2. Having a choice is better than not having a choice. The more choices one has, the freer that person is and the greater influence he or she has.

3. People make the best choice they can at the time according to their map of the world. Give them a better map and they will make a better choice.

4. People work perfectly. No one is wrong or broken. They are carrying out their strategies perfectly, but the strategies may be poorly designed and ineffective. If we consciously discover our strategies, we can change them to plans of action more useful and desirable.

5. All actions have a purpose. Actions are not random; each action is always trying to achieve something, although the actor may not be aware of what that is.

6. Every behavior has a positive intention. All our actions have at least one purpose – to achieve something that we value and that will benefit us. NLP separates the intention or purpose behind an action from the action itself. People are not their behavior. When offered a better choice of behavior to achieve their intention, they will take it.

7. The unconscious mind balances the conscious mind; it is not malicious. The unconscious is everything that is not in consciousness at the present moment. It contains all the resources we need to live in balance.

8. The meaning of the communication is not simply what is intended, but also the response you get. There are no failures in communication, only feedback. If you are not getting the result you want, change what you are doing. Take responsibility for the communication.

9. We already have all the resources we need, or if we lack resources we can create them. There are no unresourceful people, only unresourceful states of mind.

10. Mind and body form a system. They are different expressions of the one person. When we think differently, our bodies change. When we act differently, we change our thoughts and feelings.

11. We process all information through our senses. Developing our senses so that they become more acute gives us better information and helps us think more clearly.

12. Modeling successful performance leads to excellence. If one person can do something helpful, it is possible to teach it to others by example.

13. If you want to understand, act – because the learning is in the doing.

These presuppositions have led to the creation of a number of powerful strategies for change. An example is the New Behavior Generator. To illustrate, a husband and wife enjoyed bicycle riding. Each time they came to a steep hill, the husband was able to remain seated on his bike and peddle all the way up the hill, but his wife could only make it half way before she got off and walked her bike to the top. One day she asked her husband how he was able to make it to the top while seated; he explained that he put his head down and focused on his feet pushing the peddles around and around. While doing this he imagined the muscles in his legs, arms and stomach getting stronger and stronger. He pushed through the stress as he noticed the helpful exercise in his muscles. He visualized and felt the benefits to his entire body as he pumped up the hill.

As she listened to this story, she understood immediately that her strategy was entirely different. Wishing to be able to ride all the way to the top, she focused her eyes on the top of the hill. She said over and over to herself, "I think I can, I think I can." The very next time they went on a ride she copied her husband's strategy and was able to make it all the way to the top of the hill on her bike.

Another example of the power of this approach has been my losing sixty pounds without feeling like I am on a diet. The strategy that I have used has been to first clearly state my desired outcome in terms of what NLP calls a Well-Defined Outcome. The well-defined outcome starts with the question "**What do you want?**" If you want something, and you are clear about it, and committed to achieving it, the odds are that you will be successful in the end.

Of all the NLP strategies *first* is a well-defined outcome. The criteria are:

1. It must be stated positively, that is, state what you want and what you do not want.
2. It must be something that you can initiate and accomplish.
3. You must be specific about the when, where and who.
4. You must break it down into small steps.
5. It must be stated in sensory terms, that is, what will you see, hear, feel when it is accomplished, or how will you know when it is accomplished.
6. Do an ecology check using these two questions: Is there any reason that I may not want this outcome? Is the outcome congruent with my values?

The best way to learn NLP is to explore and practice the many strategies for change experienced in a group. In this approach you "do" to learn. You can read volumes about how to play tennis, but you do not begin to learn until you get on the court with racket and ball.

Anyone can learn anything by modeling. This particular insight has been very helpful to me personally. I realized that I could observe others who were able to do something that I wanted to do and simply copy their behavior and their thought processes as they successfully accomplished their tasks. As I mentioned earlier, one of my recent accomplishments has been losing sixty pounds. This weight loss came about by focusing on the fact that I wanted to get healthy. I wanted to make it to the top of the hill. I did not begin with wanting to lose weight; I wanted to get healthy.

My daughter runs triathlons. She is very healthy and I recognized that I could do much of what she does. Neuro-Linguistic Programming stresses that we state what we want rather than what we don't want. For years I conversed with myself, "I don't want to be fat." Changing the language to "I want to be healthy" has made the difference.

I use this approach with clients to help them focus on why they are coming for therapy. I help them state their therapeutic goals in positive and achievable language. Once people state an outcome positively, in sensory form (meaning what will you notice when you have achieved your goal), they are more likely to attain their goal. Reframing is a powerful intervention. For example, a woman came to me upset because she was always yelling at her husband. She stated that just about anything he said caused her to be angry. She explained that she did not want to continue yelling and losing her temper. I suggested to her a positive way to frame her desire as adopting the goal of understanding what triggered the anger in her. I suggested that she might adopt the goal of understanding the buttons that got pushed which brought forth her rage. I asked if her anger might be fueled by an experience that had been hidden from her. This helped her identify the experiences that lay behind her rage.

Ericksonian Hypnosis

The same Milton Erickson whose work inspired Neuro-Linguistic Programming was a brilliant psychiatrist who also utilized hypnosis to help people change their lives in positive ways. From Erickson I learned about the hypnotic or trance state of consciousness in everyday life. Erickson pointed out that more often than we are aware, we are in a trance. A common example can be seen in the times that I have driven from Atlanta, Georgia to Greenville, South Carolina and during the trip my mind wanders in many directions while I am driving up the Interstate. Often I waked up and realized that I had no consciousness of where I was on this trip. Yet, I drove safely up the highway while my mind generated numerous ideas. From time to time I have awakened from this trance and wondered where were the markers that would tell me where I am? This is just one illustration of the trance state.

Erickson had the ability to meet with people and utilize his voice, his posture and his presence to help the person with whom he was working to calm down, to slow down, and to move naturally and easily into a trance state. When the patient was in the trance state, Erickson made suggestions to the patient that were congruent with what the patient had decided to accomplish. He stated these suggestions as possible outcomes rather than demands. He might say, "When you leave my office and are on your way home, you may realize that you are feeling much better. You may begin to realize that your problem is going away." Erickson was a master of hypnotic suggestions to individuals that were in keeping with the individual's desires, and he did it in a way that the patient embraced.

I have learned from Milton Erickson the importance of being deliberate and conscious of the way that I use my voice. The tone, the tempo and the emphasis that the therapist uses when speaking to a client often communicate more powerfully than the particular words spoken.

The story has been told of Milton Erickson's testing this theory of tone and tempo of voice at a cocktail party. As he went through the receiving line, he spoke to the host and hostess in a delightful and soothing voice, "Oh, I just loved the fried horse meat that you offered at the party, and the frog eyes were also delicious." Erickson noticed that everyone smiled with delight at the compliments that he gave the hosts of the party. Yet, neither the hosts nor the guests heard the content of Erickson's compliment. How right he was that tone and tempo communicate in powerful, convincing ways.

I also learned from Erickson that tone and tempo often communicate something about the quality of the relationship with the individual to whom you are speaking. Just imagine the different ways that you can say a simple phrase like, "How are you?" It can be said in a slow, deliberate and warm tempo that communicates acceptance and intimacy, or it can be said in a high-pitched, loud and rapid tempo that communicates rejection. Erickson has caused me to be very deliberate about the way I use my voice in therapy sessions.

Alcoholics Anonymous

Alcoholics Anonymous is a splendid program of recovery from alcohol addiction founded by Bill Wilson. Alcoholics Anonymous centers on the twelve steps of recovery. These steps genuinely help persons who suffer from arrested development through their alcohol and drug use. A problem shared by many addicts is an enormous sense of self-absorption which creates a narcissistic bent. Their self-centeredness creates chaos and confusion for them and everyone around them. The process of breaking down this narcissism and enabling them to grow up starts with the first three steps of AA, as it is popularly called.

These steps have been described as "I can't, You can, Please do." The first step is actually a confession, "I am powerless over alcohol, and my life has become unmanageable." Number two is a faith statement:

"I have come to believe that a Power outside of myself can restore me to sanity." And the third step is, "I made a decision to turn my life and my will over to God as I understand God." These first three essential steps are followed by a moral inventory which includes a confession of one's errors, making amends and then reaching out to care for others who suffer from this disease.

I began my journey of recovery with my conversion to Christ. That conversion involved giving up drugs and alcohol plus a serious study of the Bible. It also involved my strong participation in the church. It was not until later, when my son got overpowered by alcohol, that I began going to Alcoholics Anonymous and Alanon with him. The heart of this program of recovery contains Twelve Steps that describe the experience of the earliest AA members who:

1. Admitted we were powerless over alcohol - that our lives had become unmanageable.
2. Came to believe that a Power greater than ourselves could restore us to sanity.
3. Made a decision to turn our will and our lives over to the care of God as we understood Him.
4. Made a searching and fearless moral inventory of ourselves.
5. Admitted to God, to ourselves and to another human being the exact nature of our wrongs.
6. Were entirely ready to have God remove all these defects of character.
7. Humbly asked Him to remove our shortcomings.
8. Made a list of all persons we had harmed, and became willing to make amends to them all.
9. Made direct amends to such people wherever possible, except when to do so would injure them or others.
10. Continued to take personal inventory and when we were wrong promptly admitted it.
11. Sought through prayer and meditation to improve our conscious contact with God as we understood Him, praying only for knowledge of His will for us and the power to carry that out.

12. Having had a spiritual awakening as the result of these steps, we tried to carry this message to alcoholics and to practice these principles in all our affairs.

In Alcoholics Anonymous I experienced one thing that was very different from my church experience; among these men and women I experienced a candid honesty with each other. Note the fourth, fifth and tenth steps in which the program demands complete honesty. Alcoholics Anonymous focuses on a continuous probing of the depths of one's failure, dysfunction and wreckage, which alcohol causes in the person's life and that of others. The undisciplined use of alcohol blocks relationships, creates distance, provides a shield and without alcohol many cannot be intimate.

I experienced Alcoholics Anonymous taking very seriously the biblical notion of the confession of sin to one another in order to find healing. The founder of AA, Bill Wilson, very wisely chose the way he stated the third step as turning our lives over to the power of God as we understood God. This perspective opens Alcoholics Anonymous to anyone and everyone regardless of their theology or lack thereof.

Alcoholics Anonymous has a twelve-part tradition that lays out the nature of the relationship of its members.

1. Our common welfare should come first; personal recovery depends upon AA unity.
2. For our group purpose there is but one ultimate authority—a loving God as He may express Himself in our group conscience.
3. Our leaders are but trusted servants; they do not govern.
4. The only requirement for AA membership is a desire to stop drinking.
5. Each group should be autonomous except in matters affecting other groups or AA as a whole.
6. Each group has but one primary purpose—to carry its message to the alcoholic who still suffers.
7. An AA group ought never endorse, finance, or lend the AA name to any related facility or outside enterprise, lest problems of money, property, and prestige divert us from our primary purpose.

8. Every AA group ought to be fully self-supporting, declining outside contributions.

9. Alcoholics Anonymous should remain forever non-professional, but our service centers may employ special workers.

10. AA, as such, ought never to be organized; but we may create service boards or committees directly responsible to those they serve.

11. Alcoholics Anonymous has no opinion on outside issues; hence the AA name ought never to be drawn into public controversy.

12. Our public relations policy is based on attraction rather than promotion; we need always maintain personal anonymity at the level of press, radio, and films.

Anonymity is the spiritual foundation of all our traditions, ever reminding us to place principles before personalities.

Celebrate Recovery.

Celebrate Recovery is a program designed to help people overcome the power of alcohol in a Christian frame of reference. It was developed by the Saddleback Church, founded by Dr. Rick Warren in Southern California. They describe Celebrate Recovery like this: "Celebrate Recovery, also referred to as CR, is a Christ-based approach to recovery that is a response to twelve-step programs such as Alcoholics Anonymous." It was founded in 1990 by Pastors John Baker and Rick Warren of the Saddleback Church. It aims at all "hurts, habits, and hang-ups," including but not limited to drug and alcohol addictions, sex addiction, eating disorders, and people who have been sexually abused. The founders felt that Alcoholics Anonymous was too vague in referring to God as a "higher power," and wanted a more specifically Christ-based program. Thus, "rather than turning our lives and our wills over to the power of the God of our understanding, it calls us to turn our lives and our wills over to Jesus Christ." Another difference in the Celebrate Recovery program is that each week CR begins with a meal and a prayer and a praise worship service. The worship service is followed by small groups that are separated by gender and issues being addressed.

On another night during the week small groups called "Step Studies" gather to work the steps of recovery. These small groups are organized using helpful guidelines that structure the group time in a productive way. The guidelines include rules like no cross talking, only send "I" messages and no dominating the conversation. (In other words it is my job to confess my sin, not another's.) The group proceeds with booklets in which participants, prior to the meeting, have written their responses to the questions. This small group process enables participants to continue the work beyond the weekly large group gathering. Basing the program on the twelve steps of Alcoholics Anonymous and adding the specifically Christian element has made CR a very effective program in many churches as well as in the Salvation Army's Adult Rehabilitation Centers.

Family Systems Theory

Family Systems is a look at the dynamics that go on within the whole family and the relationships in the family. Unlike Freud who sought to go inside the psyche of the individual, this therapy takes into account all the relations in a family and in the community. Murray Bowen is one of the fathers of Family Systems Theory. He noticed that in families anxiety controls and maintains the status quo of the family. Some families deal with conflict by moving closer and closer, creating what Bowen called "enmeshment." Other families deal with anxiety and discomfort by a cut off. Cut off means disowning family members who don't agree with the family rules, values and practices. Bowen also noted that individuals in families often deal with conflict by triangulation. Triangulation means, if George has a conflict with Jim, George speaks with someone else about the conflict rather than talking directly with Jim. This keeps the conflict going because those involved in the conflict never speak directly with each other. Bowen spoke about families rather than individuals because he saw families as objects of treatment. He coined the term "undifferentiated ego mass" to refer to family systems. Treatment from his point of view results in individuals becoming more differentiated. In becoming more differentiated family members are enabled to make decisions based on their own higher thinking rather than following the rules of the family.

I find this perspective extremely helpful in understanding the life of Jesus. Jesus was reared in a tradition with very strict and exacting rules. He sought to reform his culture by standing in it and speaking the truth about the social structure. His truth telling raised anxiety that eventually caused the system to put him to death.

In my family system it was understood early that children were not allowed to speak back to their parents. I felt that no one really cared what I thought or felt. The family system demanded that I meet the expectations of my parents and obey the rules and customs of our family. If I had gone for therapy with a Family Systems therapist, he/she would have discovered too many rules and expectations. First, my mother was reared in a Roman Catholic family that was wealthy and high class. She was sent to England for her schooling at the age of ten years; she lived in a convent with nuns and was educated by them through high school. She was taught that children are to be seen and not heard. Her perspective and values were transferred to our family. The Family Systems approach suggests that these values pass through one generation after another.

Biblically speaking, this perspective sheds light on how the sins of the fathers are visited on the second and third generations. When we look at these generational patterns, individuals can discover that their parents are not wholly to blame for the problem; they were unconscious victims of hand-me-down rules. They followed the patterns that had been handed down to them. In Family Systems Therapy the door opens so that different decisions about patterns of behavior are freely chosen or rejected. As members of a family differentiate, their decisions create a whole new family dynamic.

Appreciative Inquiry

Appreciative Inquiry was developed at Case Western Reserve University in 1980 by a doctoral student, David Cooperrider, and his thesis advisor, Suresh Srivastva. Fundamentally, Appreciative Inquiry is about the co-evolutionary search for the best in people, their organizations, and the relevant world around them. It suggests that we not only experience reality, we actually create it in our conversations and interactions with others. Appreciative Inquiry is a positive, strength-based approach to making changes in organizations. It includes co-creating inspiring images of what we want, and then building on positive ideas to make them happen. It means becoming more aware of our internal and external dialogues and intentionally shifting them to focus on what we want. It unleashes the positive potential within people and organizations through attention to the positive core. It suggests we build on our strengths, successes, and best practices to achieve our greatest hopes and dreams. Appreciative Inquiry is all this and more.

Appreciative Inquiry is about asking questions that focus attention on strengths and possibilities. The questions we ask ourselves and each other set the stage for and empower positive change. The What, How, When and Where questions go something like this:

What? Tell me about an experience when you felt particularly positive and empowered in your life or in work or relationships.

How? How did what you and others were doing strengthen the experience?

Where and When? Where and when have you seen the approach used in this experience used before?

Generally, the who, what, where, when, why, and how questions open up the conversation best. "Tell me about a time when . . ." is good for getting stories started. "Give me an example . . ." gets into important contextual details. "How did you feel when . . . ?" helps to expose the storyteller's core values. Avoid either-or questions or any questions that begin with the words do or does, will, can, should, or is, which normally lead to 'yes' or 'no' or very brief responses.

The questioning in Appreciative Inquiry begins with a suggestion like this: "Tell me a story about a time when you felt most effective, most passionate, when you felt the best about your work and the work of your organization." After this question is fully answered, the group is then invited to tell exactly what the employees and the organization were doing so effectively that it made a difference in the workers and in the world. This search in Appreciative Inquiry is an effort to find those values held by the majority of the group. This focus identifies what we want to do rather than search the tasks that we hate to do.

Leaders have discovered through this model that we can do more than prop up the organization; we can actually heal its problems with vision and efficiency of operation. If we focus on those things that we do well, that we feel passionate about, then the employees and the organization can more easily rise to a level of excellence. Uncovering positive attitudes and feelings increases the base of appreciation, which is the goal.

Appreciative Inquiry has had a fundamental affect both on my personal life and my counseling. Older models of therapy focused on pathology, an effort to fix what was wrong. Appreciative Inquiry concentrates on what is right, both in me and in the people that I serve.

A biblical story powerfully illustrates this approach. The story springs from the life of Jesus when a hungry crowd needed food, and a child brought five loaves and two fishes to the Master. Rather than looking at the deficiencies in what he had, the boy gave it all to Jesus and that was enough. In fact, it was more than enough. This story inspires me to value what I have and what others have. I encourage people to bring to life what they have rather than fretting over what they don't have. Very often I encounter people who make the assumption that "life will be good when . . . . when I make more money, when I get a different job, when I get the car I want." These illusions block our being present to this moment; looking for our life in the future is a form of avoidance. Healthy people look open-eyed at the present and make decisions based on what is.

Developing Capable People

Developing Capable People is a program designed by Stephen Glenn and Jane Nelson. Stephen Glenn was a brilliant and inventive man who was in recovery from alcohol; he learned much from the Twelve Step Program and focused it on people-making. He aimed to help parents become conscious of what they were seeking to nurture in their children. Too often parents, both consciously and unconsciously, shape their children to be conformable with the cultural and the family values. This approach requires more and more control over the children in order to instill conformity in them. It is desirable that children grow up to take responsibility for themselves and their choices rather than conforming or rebelling against established norms.

Stephen Glenn identified what he called "the significant seven," the core of which consisted of three attitudes and four skill sets that effective parents need to develop capable children. The attitudes that parents need to help their children develop are: 1) the attitude that I am significant, 2) the attitude that I am capable and 3) the attitude that I have influence in my life.

The four skill sets are what Glenn calls intra-psychic skills: skills in dealing with self-control and self-awareness; skills in relating to others, e.g., empathy and communication; systemic skills which enables them to deal with the family system, the neighborhood system, the school system and the government. The final skill set puts together all the behavioral skills, the skills required to make good judgments to become capable and well adapted people.

The other base of Glenn's training concerns Builders and Barriers in relationships. These Builders and Barriers are actions and words that create respect and enhance capabilities for human interaction or barriers that block this achievement. Here is how these contrasting actions line up:

Builders	*vs.*	**Barriers**
Checking		Assuming
Exploring		Rescuing/Explaining
Encouraging/Inviting		Directing
Celebrating		Expecting
Respecting		Adultisms

Glenn designed this program to be conducted two hours a week for ten weeks. In weekly class sessions the concepts are presented; following class, parents are divided into groups to practice the exercises to help internalize the ideas. The presentation of material and the group experience enable the parents to gain skills and deeper insights into how the system works.

Through the years I found myself using this rich perspective in individual and family therapy. Often parents need to understand more clearly what to emphasize in order to empower their children. As they continue in the program, they begin to say that they are on a journey to developing capable people. In the training the parents are changed so that they can, perhaps, rear their children to become capable adults. Couples often report that the training in developing capable people has changed their relationship not only with their children but also with each other and has increased their effectiveness in their vocation.

These insights have certainly helped me deal with my issues. In times of struggle and anxiety with my son I have seen how my anxiety makes me want to control the situation. My anxiety pushes me to make demands on him. Subscribing to this perspective has enabled me to treat him with respect, to interact with him through checking out what I think he is saying and exploring with him, rather than directing him. This approach has a better outcome than efforts to direct or control because once a child is out of diapers, we parents are never in complete control again, if we ever were. I have to keep my respect for him even when his choices are painful to both of us. Living by the insights of this program helps people who are seeking to have integrity in their relationships.

The Enneagram

The Enneagram is a rich and helpful study of human personality. It combines spiritual and psychological insights that describe both the strengths and challenges of different personality types. I can recommend it as a worthwhile study for anyone seeking growth and personal development.

The system describes nine personality styles along with the strengths and challenges of each. The styles are based on the dominance of different centers of influence and temperament that shape personality. The centers of influence are the head, heart and gut, or thinking, feeling and doing. The temperaments are assertive, withdrawn and compliant styles. Given these centers of influence and temperaments there are three head styles, three heart styles and three gut styles. To learn more about this powerful tool visit the Rios and Hudson web site. (http://www.enneagraminstitute.com)

Exploring One's Inner Child

In preparation to become a therapist and counselor, I became aware of a leader in the field of the inner child, John Bradshaw. I once watched a video in which he was teaching people how to work with their inner child. The large audience had gathered to learn from him about lingering childhood hurts and hopes. He invited the audience to get relaxed, to close their eyes and to take several deep breaths. In this relaxed state he invited them to return to that childhood era of their lives and to picture the little child who was still living within them.

He then encouraged the participants to look into the eyes of that little child, to put their arms around that child and hold him or her close. He instructed them to make promises to that child. He suggested that they promise the child that they would always be its advocate and that they would never abandon him or her. As the camera panned the audience, I noticed tears flowing from the eyes of many of the participants. Others were leaning back in their chairs expressing sighs of relief. It was evident that this intervention was both powerful and meaningful to those who were encountering their inner child.

Working with the inner child has been useful in working with people who have struggled with old patterns that control their lives. I remember a supervisor, Gloria White, who guided me as I prepared for licensure as a mental health professional. Gloria often asked me, "How does little Robby feel about this or that?" She taught me the importance of being little Robby's advocate.

Through the years I have worked with numerous people whose wounded child feared abandonment. I have worked with others whose inner child was terribly afraid of criticism, abuse and punishment. Therapeutically, it is crucial for the adult part of the self to make promises to the child within the self. The adult self makes promises to never abandon the child, to always be the child's advocate.

I sometimes encourage clients to picture themselves as a strong adult holding the hand of their vulnerable little inner child. I ask them to visualize themselves crossing a very busy street where brakes squeal and horns blow; I encourage them to hold the child's hand as they wade through the traffic. Life is often filled with clutter and confusion and dangerous moments when the child within needs a secure hand in order to cope. Often, little children have not learned to deal effectively with these experiences, and they need confidence and reassurance of the adult that lives beside them.

This inner child is the seat of our feelings. Too often when we are fearful, we are filled with anxiety that controls our functioning. This fear easily leads to self-defeating and destructive patterns of behavior. The process of advocating for, holding and protecting the vulnerable little child can help us to be more rational and healthy in our thinking. Encouraging the child within enables us to engage in life in a more productive and redemptive manner.

Business Administration Degree

I majored in business administration in the undergraduate school at the University of South Carolina. Through those studies I learned a great deal about marketing, salesmanship, business law, accounting, and other basic business practices. In my career I've been a part owner and operator of a travel agency, which included a great deal of selling, promotion, planning and customer service. I also owned a private practice in pastoral counseling. Through these varied experiences, I have derived an understanding of business management and consequently have an appreciation of those who have the total responsibility for managing the different facets of a business. This understanding has been helpful to me in my counseling practice because I have had numerous clients who were involved in both corporate and family businesses. I believe my understanding of business helps me speak a language that offers guidance to the person who is struggling with issues in his or her work life. A person's work life has a profound impact on family life and on one's individual, spiritual and emotional life. Thus, work and work issues form an important aspect of counseling and therapy.

Participating and Leading Small Groups

Through the years I have participated in and led many small groups. During my training in pastoral care and counseling, I participated in small groups. The principles I learned in this training have helped me to understand what makes a small group effective. I learned, for example, that the consciousness of the leader regarding his or her own psychological and spiritual makeup greatly impacts the group. Many times what is going on with the leader affects the dynamics of a small group. I learned how group members from the very beginning learn how to attach themselves to persons who will protect and nurture them. No matter what the stated purpose of the group, these interpersonal dynamics are always present.

My original training in leading small groups was psychoanalytically oriented. My trainers gave a significant amount of attention to the ways group members sought to attach themselves to the leader and to each other. In small groups I have experienced both the closeness and conflict that goes on between group members. These dynamics are often similar to, and sometimes they are carbon copies of, the dynamics that go on with these same persons outside of the group. Actually, attending to these patterns of behavior in the group offers a richer, lifelike experience than can be achieved in individual counseling or therapy.

I have learned that as a leader, therapist or group facilitator, I must be able to emotionally move in and out of the group. It is essential for me to join with members in the group deeply enough for them to feel safe, while at the same time I must maintain enough objectivity and separation from the group to discern the dynamics that are unfolding. An image of how this leadership unfolds can be compared to my place in a church sanctuary with a balcony. I can be in the balcony or on the main floor or at other sites as I choose. In the balcony I am observing what's going on in the relationships below on the main floor; I can come down from the balcony and join in the dynamics that are taking place. As a facilitator it is important to maintain this constant movement in and out, to be both part of and separate from the group.

A Brief Summary

All these experiences in different streams have deeply affected my life. I have found ways to face myself honestly, to listen sympathetically to my inner child and to make choices that have enriched and changed my life. As a consequence of these good things that have come to me through these various channels, I truly want to pass on to others what I have learned in some of the hard struggles of life.

CHAPTER ELEVEN

My Theory of Healing Therapy

✽

ONE OF THE MOST CHALLENGING PROBLEMS that I have faced is how to conceptualize my understanding of what I do in therapy. All the experiences that I have had in my past form a pool from which I draw each time I meet someone in a counseling session. The insights and intuitions that I draw on today have been instilled in me by my experiences, my reading through the years and the role models that I observed. Another aspect of the healing art that I practice comes through spiritual direction. Spiritual direction helps people join their search for mental health with their faith. I once had a conversation with a friend of mine about the relationship of therapy to spiritual direction. I asked him, "What is the difference between spiritual direction and pastoral counseling?"

He replied, "In spiritual direction we ask the question, 'Where is God in the ordinary events of my life? What is God saying to me through them?' In pastoral counseling we ask how can we deal with problematic events in a healthy way?" Though these emphases represent two different approaches to life, though they overlap, spiritual direction does not do therapy, and pastoral counseling does not focus on spiritual direction. Both of these perspectives have special tasks and both seem important to me. Both of these arts have had a significant place in my life.

In counseling I hope to offer what I have learned from life, study and the practice of ministry in a way that will be healing. I am deeply grateful for all those who have shared what they have discovered with me, and I constantly attempt to pass on to others what I have found to be valuable.

My life has been filled with great joy and serious pain. I want to share my insights and learning in a way that will assist others in life's battles. What has been most helpful to me has been hearing in the stories of others things that resonate with my own story. Nothing is more revealing or more powerful than hearing an honest story. This identification with another not only reflects our own problem, it also helps us know that we are not alone in our battles.

Telling life stories offers healing both to the storyteller and the listener. As we tell others our stories, we revisit our sources of trauma and learning. Socrates said that the unexamined life is not worth living. Telling stories helps us to glean lessons from the most painful experiences that we have gone through as well as the most satisfying. Again and again, I have received healing from hearing and sharing stories.

Communication

I believe that the single most important element in healing and liberation for a person flows from good, effective communication. I have studied the model that Sherod Miller developed and found it very helpful. His model places two parties in the encounter: a speaker and a listener. He states specific listening and speaking behaviors. For one person to communicate effectively with another, each must practice these speaking and listening skills. To speak clearly, the speaker must express fully an awareness of the issue being dealt with. To do so involves naming the issue and describing the facts, thoughts and feelings that he or she has about the issue. Finally, the speaker must state clearly what is desired, what actions he or she is requesting.

Communication is signally important because it has a deep bearing on the realities of everyday life. We get an idea of the power of words when we read in the Bible that God spoke creation into being. God said, "Let there be light and there was light." That is amazing power! Spoken words possess great power when they become a part of our lives, sometimes with positive results and sometime with negative results.

The Bible also speaks of Christ as the Word of God made flesh. God communicated through Christ who God is and what God does in the world. Communication is a process of sending and receiving information. In order for accurate communication to take place, it must be transmitted and received with an opportunity for clarification. Only clarification makes it possible for the hearer to receive what the speaker is saying.

I emphasize communication because effective communication is essential to our emotional and spiritual health. Good communication does not mean that we have agreement when the communication is understood. It simply means that we understand what the other has said and what was meant.

Clarification through questions and feedback is essential for this understanding. For example, I have a minister friend with whom I disagree; I disagree with his views, his sermons and the values he holds. He and I think very differently about the Christian faith. As I listen to his views and process them in my mind, I discover more clearly what I myself think, feel and believe. My understanding of his faith clarifies my own view; even though we disagree on many issues, we understand each other's positions and that we hold different views; in spite of our differences we can be in a healthy relationship. Communication means clarity of understanding, not agreement.

Communication contains both verbal and nonverbal content. These two types of communication are descriptions of manifest and latent content in communication. The latent aspect of communication is nonverbal and accounts for about 90% of what is expressed. This nonverbal communication provides the relational quality of what is being communicated. The verbal content accounts for about 10% of what is expressed. This manifest aspect of communication also requires verbal clarification because words are used in so many different ways.

When a family is rife with anger, many family members feel isolated, cut off and uncared for. When I talk with each of the family members in an anger-laden home, it becomes clear to me that each person feels rejected and marginalized. The patterns of communication born from anger and mistrust point to underlying battles that create resentment and end up in confusion. These dysfunctional patterns trap family members and shape their outlook and responses. The challenge of these poor patterns of interaction requires that each member learn to put the latent content of the communication into nonjudgmental words.

Empathy

The experiences of my life provide me with the empathy that I feel when I either share my story or listen to another's story. I seldom hear another person's story that does not have a piece of me in it. True healing demands empathy. When a person truly understands what another person is going through, they do not offer easy solutions to complex situations. From their own experience they know how difficult it is to endure the pain and uncertainty that the sufferer feels. Being empathetic and compassionate to a person in pain provides the support that a struggler needs.

Each week I listen to stories told by persons who are caring for loved ones with diseases like Alzheimer's. Most of the caregivers simply listen to the story of pain without interrupting because they know that they cannot banish pain with words. What they can do is listen with care and compassion. We cannot feel other people's pain, but we can recognize and understand their distress and we can be there for them. Being present to another is the core of empathy.

Patterns of Poor Communication

When I began this long journey of recovery and authenticity, I was not aware of the variegated layers of my problem. I did not recognize the array of feelings within me and all the decisions that I had made and the responses that I had chosen in order to survive. The people who come to me for help often are not aware of their own self-defeating behavior. Because they are not aware of their mental habits, I seek to discover the destructive patterns in their lives. I wonder with them, sometimes aloud, where each of these blockages came from.

I worked with a couple recently who realized that they had a pattern of endless conflict. The husband, for example, jokingly poked fun at his wife and criticized her. She immediately exploded in fits of rage, yelling at him and calling him names. She came to see me with the hope that I could help her get control of her feelings. She was genuinely concerned about her behavior and longed to be freed from this pattern of rage. As we explored her situation, she described how she had grown up in a conflicted home where there were mountains of criticism. She brought the wounds from her family of origin into the marriage. Her husband had come from a family in which he had three brothers who were constantly competing by making fun of each other. Her husband's banter and kidding reminded her of the criticisms and put-downs that she received from her mother. Just as she had dealt with her mother, she resorted to anger and rage to protect herself from her husband. This rage was an overreaction to the conflict going on between them.

As far as the inner psyche is concerned, there is no such thing as an overreaction. The present situation gives rise to the wound from earlier experience in a way that the individual is transported to that old pain from the past. When this happens, the individual is no longer emotionally present but instead is flooded with feelings from the past.

As we explored the dynamics that each of them brought from their families of origin, they learned to relate in more respectful ways. As they learned to be aware and live with appreciation and respect, their relationship improved and grew stronger. Soon they could recognize when past experience was triggered that drained their capacity to be present to themselves and to each other.

Unconditional Acceptance

I seek to offer unconditional acceptance to every person with whom I meet; many have never had an experience of unconditional love, that is, love without strings attached. So often gifts and services are given in relationships with unvoiced expectations. If you enter a store to purchase an article, you look at the item and on it a tag or label states the price. You know how much you will pay for the purchase, but in relationships the price is not revealed and there is an unconscious expectation nearly always present.

As a therapist I have an expectation that the person I am seeking to help will respond positively. This expectation colors the way I speak, the way I listen and the suggestions that I make to a person seeking help.

Creating Awareness in Another

Creating an awareness in a person's mind is the first step toward a change in behavior. We cannot deliberately change our patterns if we are unaware of them. With respect to communication we often say, "A person cannot, not communicate." The reason? Everything communicates. As clients enter my office, their dress, the speed of their walk, where they choose to sit and how they sit tells me something about them. I listen to the tone of their voice, become aware of their facial expressions, attend the dynamics of our encounter and all of these communicate something of the person to me.

I observe both the verbal and nonverbal content of my client's communication. Often what a person says verbally and what I observe in their behavior are incongruent. This means that the message that is being communicated nonverbally contradicts the message communicated verbally. For instance, someone says, in a very loud and intrusive voice, "I love you." The tone of voice does not match the content of what is said. In a setting like this, the listener or hearer always believes the nonverbal message. When you ask a person a question like, "How do you feel about your relationship with your daughter?" – the words may be, "I feel really good about our relationship; we get along just fine." But as you observe their behavior, you notice the girl hangs her head, turns her eyes toward the floor and draws back in her chair; you may even notice that both hands are twitching. All these behaviors tell something about this person.

These insights originally came to me from my family of origin. Very often the words that were spoken and the behavior that followed contradicted what was said. This situation taught me the importance of interpreting both the verbal and nonverbal messages passed between us. Intuitively, I knew that the customs in the family were not stated clearly. The expectations of the family system came out nonverbally with a stare, a tone of voice or a withdrawal or an attack. After we were married, my wife had difficulty interacting with my family because she didn't know the insider language and often took statements at face value. Ignorance of family patterns of communication often makes the outsider feel ignored or estranged.

Freud discovered that human beings repress or suppress thoughts and feelings that are unacceptable to them. Repression removes them from consciousness. These unacceptable, unwanted thoughts and feelings find expression nonverbally. So in a therapy session a husband may say to his wife, "Oh honey, you know that you didn't make me angry; you know that I never get angry with you. I love you, and everything you do is fine with me." But the tone of his voice and the expression on his face made it clear that the speaker was very angry but unable to admit it. Even in his denial, he became even angrier and still could not see his rage.

Once I was in a therapy group with a minister who could not face his anger. The group was confronting him about it. His Christian tradition had taught him that it was unacceptable to be angry. He said to the group, "Oh, I'm not angry," but as he spoke, his teeth were grinding, his voice was very high pitched and both of his fists were clenched. But he repeatedly insisted, "I am not angry!" The verbal and nonverbal messages he was sending certainly did not match.

Pointing the Path to God

As a pastoral counselor my perspective and beliefs are formed by my faith tradition which points to the redemptive power of a loving God. I am painfully aware that many people have been deeply hurt by and even abused by churches. They have often felt controlled and manipulated by an authoritative appeal or directive in the name of God. Because of these abuses, in counseling sessions I encounter people who are seeking healing but are dubious about too many references to God. Rather than offering them religious principles to live by or solutions from Scripture that are supposed to fix their problem, I first attempt to connect significantly with them on a personal level. One method that helps me connect is the exploration of their childhood experiences. I choose this approach because memories of childhood are at a distance and therefore less threatening. Also, what happened in their childhood still influences them today. I also wonder with them about their joys and disappointments, the high points and low points in their lives. Behind this exploration what goes unstated is the belief that God desires to connect with us in everything that has happened and is happening to us. When I am able to connect with them, I begin to explore the little child that still lives in them. People are empowered to stand back from their present experience and look at the experiences that formed their lives; this experience of childhood creates safety in them. At this point I urge them to give unconditional love and acceptance to that child within so that the true self may emerge. I always hope that they consciously experience the reality of a present, loving God. I do not offer easy answers to complex questions. I believe that when persons connect with their true self, others and life, healing begins to occur.

Removing the Blockage

In my sessions I also seek to help people discover the blockage in their lives and point out ways that they may get through these barriers to growth. In the process of living we all develop strategies that assist us in adapting to our circumstances. These adaptations originate in early life and later become defenses. Even though our lives change, we continue to utilize the same strategies that we originally learned to harmonize our lives, even though the context of our life has radically changed. My father's relationship to me illustrates this point. He was very angry and often attacked me for the slightest breaking of one of his rules. In order to adapt to his excessive anger, I learned how to distance myself from him and to deny what was happening to me; I defended myself with denial but stored up my deep hurt and hid my wound. This adaptation to life later functioned as a defense mechanism when I was rebuked or chastised. My father's abuse created a pattern that I relied on to deal with all authority figures who overreacted to me. I assumed that they had no capacity to understand or to connect with me.

I developed this strategy for a very good reason – it worked. At least, it worked effectively for me when I was a child, but later in life it created a barrier to positive relationships with authority figures. My response illustrates a neurotic pattern that operates unconsciously and automatically. When these patterns become disruptive, people often use the occasion to seek help in making significant changes.

On the ceiling of the Sistine Chapel there is a painting that depicts one hand reaching down and another reaching up; this image depicts my role in counseling – helping the person reaching up for help to discover that there is another hand reaching down to him or her. I believe that there is a hand reaching to all of us; I have touched it and it has touched me. The greatest gift that any of us has to offer is pointing others to the path of hope. My life is continuously enriched as I have the privilege of helping others find glimpses of liberation.

Great Respect and Esteem

I seek to grant all my clients the respect and esteem that they deserve. What I hope to do with every person is condensed in the words of Max Ehrmann in Desiderata: "You are a child of the universe, no less than the trees and the stars; you have a right to be here. And whether or not it is clear to you, no doubt the universe is unfolding as it should."

I have a great deal of respect for individuals who muster up enough courage to enter my office and seek help. To open oneself to another human being takes extraordinary courage. When the door opens and the client sits down, I feel a deep urge to symbolically take off my shoes because I believe that I am on holy ground. So how do I behave when I notice that I am on holy ground? First, I have a great confidence in silence and waiting. Parker Palmer suggests that silence helps us to encounter the soul. He sometimes describes the soul as a wild animal that hides deep in the woods. If you run noisily into the woods seeking an encounter with that animal, it will run away and hide. But if you sit quietly, respectfully waiting on that animal, it will come out and show itself to you. Slowly, timidly and carefully the soul will appear when we wait quietly. So to communicate respect, I patiently wait on another person's readiness to reveal his or her hiddenness; when that happens, healing begins.

When I am waiting, I refuse to ask emotionally loaded questions. I am careful to refrain from seeking information driven by my own curiosity. It is so important to wait for people to speak about what they need to give voice to. In waiting I take a relaxed posture, a soft, caring, non-intrusive tone of voice, and I sometimes seek to match their posture and even their breathing patterns and words. I pay attention to the language they use and use it as I speak to them in an effort to communicate in their frame of reference.

In my relationship with clients I seek to communicate the message that they are the expert on their lives and their experiences. I refrain from offering interpretations or expert commentary on the material they present to me.

I suppose that respect is important to me because of the people in my life who have shown me genuine respect. Gloria White, a supervisor trainer whom I have already mentioned as an expert in her field, gave me astonishing respect. Leigh Conver, another supervisor and trainer, also offered me unquestionable respect. The one person that I have always depended on for respect has been my wife. She not only has given me respect, she has earnestly traveled my journey of healing with me. I could name a long list of folks from whom I have been shown respect, but I will let one more person enter this sacred circle, T. Neese, my faculty advisor at Columbia Seminary. Can you imagine what respect would mean in some of the troublesome situations in your life?

Be a Companion on the Journey

When I am offering therapy, I want to be with persons in the issues that engage them in the present. My calling is to be with people who are on life's journey, especially when they are passing through darkness, desolation and uncertainty. I want to hold their hand and walk with them into their deepest fears. My idea of a counselor requires me to be on the journey with them. As I journey with them, my feelings and beliefs give rise to empathy for their pain and understanding of their quandary. My journey and their journey are different, but they are connected and disconnected at the same time. This realization constantly reminds me that we can be with each other without projecting our experience on the other as if we knew exactly what the other is thinking or feeling or experiencing. Rather than having a one to one unity, we have a parallel unity because something in our two different experiences is similar. I am always aware that my experience is my experience, and sharing my experience may give rise to insight for another person.

As a companion on the journey I want to be a non-anxious presence with other people. Problems occur when we over-identify with another person. A worse problem arises when we try to be a savior. I do not desire to save a person; I am not the savior. My desire is to work with and for persons, but the true work must be done by them because only they can take responsibility for themselves and make the necessary changes. Over-identification is manifest in our thinking that we know exactly what their problem is and what they should do. This leads to our projecting our point of view on their situation. This error can significantly interfere with people's ability to do their own work. The best we have to offer is being on the journey with them while we are seriously on our own journey. We should never take responsibility for others or intrude into their space.

Celebrate Victories Together

The primary tool that I bring to counseling is myself – my pain, my failure, my healing and my hope for myself and others. Dick Felder images therapy as a symphony of selves. Healing requires learning and growth on the part of the therapist and client alike. Therapy is not like performing surgery or dispensing pills. Neither is it like coaching or teaching because it involves something very different from teaching information or skills. Good therapy involves getting into the flow of life with the client. Socrates describes this as floating down the river on opposite ends of a log. There is an interchange and a process of learning that is taking place for both therapist and patient. We are both learning, changing and growing as we engage each other in the challenges of life. The client's life, both past and present, provides the story line for the journey of both therapist and patient as they work together navigating the stream of life and gather experience from the journey. Therapist and client share the disappointments and joys experienced along the way. For me it is a time of great celebration when one of my insights is valuable to another person. I celebrate the other person's discoveries as I celebrate my own. Together we celebrate what each of us has discovered about life. When therapy is successful, both therapist and client become better adapted to life.

I find another kind of connectedness that bears fruit in my life – being part of a group where honest and open sharing takes place. I encourage my clients to participate in a faith community like a small group. The Alzheimer's group that I facilitate, the Thursday morning prayer breakfast, the Tuesday evening addiction group and the Sunday worship – all these group experiences nourish and empower my life. Working with clients, frequent conversations with trusted friends and daily devotions with my wife strengthen my faith, hope and love. I cannot create these experiences in solitude; I need interaction with others.

Give Bountiful Permissions

As an aspect of my approach, I give bountiful permissions – I give people permission to try, to fail, and to try again. Too many have grown up with rules of behavior that do not make room for failure. From the time we enter the first grade, we are constantly given feedback on what we should do and not do and which rules we have broken. The red X's that I got on papers returned to me are indelibly stamped in my memory. At home I also got an abundance of negative feedback, documenting what I had done wrong. My father's voice still rings in my ears, "Robby, what were you thinking? Are you that stupid?" This criticism created in me an inhibiting fear of making mistakes. My mistakes drew criticism and ridicule while successes went unnoticed. I have learned that mistakes can be life's greatest teacher.

As an alcoholic in recovery, I know that hitting the wall or having a major upset can lead to sweeping changes. Most often humans make changes when they can do nothing else to relieve their pain. We try to make dysfunctional patterns work until we have no strength left in us and then we open up to new possibilities. I have heard it said that an airplane flying from point A to point B is off track 95% of the time. By noticing the degree to which the plane is off course and making adjustments, the pilot navigates the aircraft. When we are changing course in life, we should make adjustments in flight and do so with a nonjudgmental attitude.

Life is a school in which we learn most from our failures. If we are unable to accept failures, we persist in a defensive reaction that blocks learning from our mistakes. Avoidance like this leaves us struggling over and over with the same challenges in our dysfunctional path. I know a man whose mother constantly told him that he was smart and good. He internalized 'smart' and 'good' as his identity. As a result of this conditioning, he was not free to be fully himself. He judged that behaviors that did not meet the mark of 'smart and good' were totally forbidden. As he spoke of his conditioning, he identified it as a hidden life. In therapy he began to embrace the richness and fullness of the person he actually was. Acceptance set him free to learn and grow from all his life experiences. He said to me, "I no longer feel a need to label myself as either 'smart' or 'good'." He had been liberated to accept his life as it unfolded without feeling compelled to make a judgment of its character.

Sharing My Faith Honestly

Sharing and discussing one's faith is important for nurture, grounding and relationship building. I seek to demonstrate the faith that has transformed my life not only in words but in my actions. I speak with clients of God the Creator, the love of Christ and the presence of the Spirit in our lives today. This is my credo, what I believe: I believe that people are made in the image of God. Among other things, this means that life lived with openness evolves toward strength and health driven by God's Spirit within. If this were not true, organisms would not survive the ever-changing circumstances of life. God as the Creator makes life possible, as the Sustainer God grants sunshine, water and air, and God the Redeemer initiates all that is healing – food, love and purpose. Paul Tillich speaks of God as "the Ground of our Being" and everything that exists is rooted in this ground.

Based on this affirmation, therapy is a way of helping a person get through the unrecognized defenses and the automated patterns of thought and emotion which block the individual from being consciously present to what is going on in daily life. These defenses and patterns of thought have been developed as a survival necessity. In my practice I try to demonstrate that through faith and change, life can be transformed.

I love my work because the insights that I have discussed have transformed my life and have given me peace and fullness of life. The Christian story of the gracious God enables me to believe in the goodness and purposefulness of life. The depth of love that I have experienced through Jesus Christ has convinced me that unconditional love and acceptance are powerful enough to heal and transform everyone. In me, shame and guilt have only created anger and resistance, and I am convinced guilt has had the same effect on other people. When I meet with clients, I look for the positive intentions that lie behind their destructive behavior.

The other crucial dimension of faith for me is the experience of community. I experience the presence of God through others, especially when I hear their stories and share mine with them. There is a parallel here with Alcoholics Anonymous. The point is that we are not alone, we are not so different in make-up and we deeply crave the same things. Mental health specialists say that isolation creates emotional instability. We are social beings and need the interactions of others on the journey of faith. We will never walk alone and we will never be left to our own devices because Jesus has promised, "I am with you always, even to the end of the age."

The Apostle Paul admonishes us with these words: "Rejoice with those who rejoice, weep with those who weep. Live in harmony with one another; do not be haughty, but associate with the lowly; do not claim to be wiser than you are." (Romans 12:15-16, NRSV)

Become a Fully Functioning Person

I have been writing out of my deepest knowledge and experience of healing and wholeness. I want now to set forth what I think a healthy, mature, developing person looks like. When I begin defining the fully functioning person, I'm first reminded that people are very different. My thought about fully functioning people nudges me to say that these people have been liberated to reach their highest potential. People have different personalities, different emotional, physical and spiritual influences shaping their lives. They also have different levels of intelligence and capability. In order for an individual to be fully functioning, he or she must draw on all of their internal resources. Theoretically speaking, if human beings from birth to adulthood get what is needed along the developmental pathway, they will emerge as fully functioning persons, at least as fully functioning as they can be. On this pathway all of us meet with challenges that create defenses and leave us with wounds; getting beyond these defenses leads to health and happiness.

I believe in a community of faith where people experience acceptance and challenges to become all that they can be; there is a power present that helps us all to transcend the wounds and defenses that enslave us. When I say "a community of faith," I am not speaking only of a church, synagogue, mosque or temple, but groups like AA and Alanon where loving acceptance prevails, making them healing communities. Add to this the awareness that fully functioning for one individual may be very different from fully functioning for another. For instance, I once knew a family who had two sons. One son was severely retarded mentally. The other son had a very high IQ and excelled at every pursuit he followed. Interestingly, the son with mental retardation reached his potential much earlier than his more intelligent brother. The boy with mental retardation was a happy, well-adjusted man who worked as a janitor in a local school. He accomplished his work with a positive, can-do attitude. His younger brother, who seemingly had far more potential, had great difficulty choosing which direction to follow. He suffered emotional and spiritual blocks as well as unrealistic expectations of himself and others.

Each of us is born with certain abilities, callings and gifts. Some of us naturally have better motor skills. Others are born with exceptional bodies and possess a strong athletic prowess. Others inherit greater intellectual capacities. A fully functioning human being is one who identifies and utilizes all of his or her natural abilities. We are called to identify our God-given gifts and develop them to the best of our power. Attending to these tasks is how individuals become fully functioning.

The principles describing fully functioning people also apply to families, to leaders, to teachers and to politicians. Dr. Frank Harrington, a minister with whom I had the privilege of working, was himself a great leader. He believed that leadership could be developed in people who were born with a natural gift for leading; he strongly believed that leaders are born and not taught. He seemed to have a special talent for recognizing those persons and guiding them in the productive use of their gifts.

CHAPTER TWELVE

Looking Back, Looking in, Looking Forward

❋

IF LIFE IS FOR LEARNING, I have completed a number of both entry level and graduate school classes. Of all these courses I have had in the University of Life, one stands out above all the others; I have learned the master key to living – – gratitude. Gratitude is the response of appreciation for who we are and what has happened to us in the various stages of our lives.

My Past

As I review my life, there are a number of things for which I'm grateful. I am grateful for the privilege of being, for my parents and my grandmother and my aunt Blanche. I'm grateful for the endowment of human consciousness that enables me to look out at the world, to embrace it and to find my place in the great unfolding of the universe. "I am a child of the universe, I have a right to be here and the universe is unfolding as it should." What could be greater than to be born into a world like this with the opportunity to face challenges, overcome obstacles and to make the discovery of freedom, wholeness and joy?

I am grateful for my wife Jane and our two children and all that we have shared and learned together. I am grateful for my three grandchildren and the opportunities that I have to be a part of their lives. I am also deeply grateful for my two loving sisters, Lynn and Patty. They have both loved me and supported me through all of my years. I cannot imagine growing up without them.

The abusive practice of my father not only affected me, but it had a frightening effect on my sisters also. Both of them were traumatized by my father's erratic behavior. When Lynn was reading the original manuscript of this book, she recalled how she and my mother had stood outside the bathroom door during one of his beatings. Lynn then told me how she felt helpless and ashamed that she could not protect me from my father's wrath. How fortunate I have had compassionate sisters who felt for me when I was young and now speak honestly with me about the rearing we shared.

In good times and in bad times we have had each other. We have laughed together and cried together through many of life's challenges. For us as for many siblings our family life growing up was good, bad and at times painful. We enjoyed many fun family trips to Pawleys Island, Nantucket, New York, Nassau and other places. We enjoyed great times at our family lake and mountain houses. We had good family time on our cabin cruiser on Lake Hartwell. We also had painful times when our parents were drinking, fighting and putting out shame and guilt for minor mistakes.

All of our life experience informs and makes us who we are. As adults we have spent vacations and holidays together. These are occasions that we cherish and look forward to.

In addition to my gratitude for the privilege of being, and all the good things that have come into my life, especially my siblings, I am also grateful for the negative things, the trying things that have found their way into my life. First of all, I am grateful for my family of origin. In writing about my family, I am aware that I have emphasized the conflict, the struggle and the abuse that I went through. How could I be grateful for that? Those experiences have been the bread and butter of my growth; they have demanded that I look at my life and the patterns of thought and behavior I adopted and change them into positive, healthy thoughts and actions. In a sense, all the suffering that I went through in my family has given me a deep appreciation and understanding of others passing through similar circumstances. So I'm thankful for all that has happened in my life because it has given me the opportunity to grow up, to deal honestly with myself and to become the person that I am today.

Second, I am grateful for the slide into alcoholism and the deliverance that I have experienced. Again, it was my addiction to alcohol that led me into the deep darkness of my unexamined soul and shook me to the core of my being. From that foundational position, I began to make my way back to sanity and wholeness. Without my alcohol addiction, I possibly would never have learned the most basic principles of life that came to me through AA. Certainly, I am not proud of the pain and hurt my alcoholism caused people close to me, but my alcoholism forced me to face the truth of my life that I was indeed an alcoholic. Accepting this foundational truth helped me grow and break the old patterns that enslaved me.

Third, I am grateful for all the struggles that Jane and I have gone through. In all our struggles Jane consistently showed me compassion, acceptance and love. She has demonstrated to me the traits that I so desired in my wild life. We went through many trying experiences with Robert: his struggle to learn, his addiction to drugs and alcohol, and his numerous failures to adjust to reality. Through all of this Jane served as a stalwart power to keep our family ship on course and to keep it moving forward.

Fourth, I am grateful for Robert. I appreciate the gift of Robert because he has challenged my love in every aspect of his life. Over and over again I had to learn how to love, how to forgive and how to endure the pain of seeing him struggling in an emotional prison. The gift from those painful experiences has been empathy with every person who walks into my life, especially those who walk through the doors of pain with their child's problems. I am in no place to judge any person or to condemn any person for their aberrant behavior. Did not Pope Francis say something like that?

Fifth, my daughter and I have an amazing relationship. In so many ways Jane Gower and I are so much alike. I am grateful that she is open to whatever I have to share with her about my lessons from life. On her own, she is forever seeking the next step, the new adventure or the mystery that she feels a need to explore. I'm honored that she and her husband, Mark, have taken the parenting class that I teach and have used it to great benefit in their family. Her way of facing into life inspires me because she engages life in the same way that she competes in triathlons – damn the torpedoes, full speed ahead. I delight also in the grandchildren she and Mark have presented to Jane and me: Mary Elizabeth and Mark.

My Present

I am grateful not only for the things that have happened in my past and the growth that has occurred because of them, I am also grateful for the present. I have learned that life is always lived in the present – – the place in which I stand now, the environment that surrounds me at this moment and the people who come into my life this day. I see every event, every thought and every person as sources of gratitude and thanksgiving. I delight in the things that are happening in this era of my life. After seven decades my feeling of appreciation has only deepened.

In this present moment I celebrate my vocation. I can think of nothing greater to be involved in, nothing more fulfilling than to engage people every day and listen to their stories of pain and frustration and hopelessness and then have the opportunity to share with them new possibilities for their lives. What a joy to see them take charge of their lives, learn to make good decisions and become transformed. Helping people to stop hurting may be the beginning, but the big payoff is a new life that is filled with hope. Hallelujah! Thanks be to God for the calling placed on my life.

In the specific present that I'm living today, I am part of a great community of loving people. Shallowford Presbyterian Church is not a perfect church, but it is a loving church and a church open to growth. I have the opportunity to work with a dynamic minister, with a powerful youth leader, with an exceptionally talented choir director and with a number of groups in this congregation. There is nothing in my present setting that can destroy my sense of gratitude for being here, now.

I have mentioned before that I lead an Alzheimer's group. Week after week we gather, tell our stories and share each other's pain. Through this period of the long goodbye, those caring for their loved ones are particularly vulnerable. They often have feelings of desperation in which they are reaching for straws, for anything that seems to offer stability. I see my role as continuing to offer support and caring for these who are in a most vulnerable posture.

There is such a fulfillment for me and I believe for all those who participate in this group. We are discovering what it means to be the

Body of Christ on earth. If one of us hurts, all of us hurt; if one of us is fearful, we all share the fear together. Whatever is the substance of one person's life becomes the substance of our life together. So I am grateful to be involved with people who are finding light in their darkness and strength for their deepest struggle.

I go to the men's prayer group every Thursday morning. In this group we have breakfast together, we review the needs of the congregation and we pray. It's simple, but it is so important to my life. Nothing else compares to the openness and honesty that these men exhibit toward each other. In this group there is appreciation for those who come from very different places in life. The group hosts people from twenty-five to ninety-five years of age and all have different issues in their lives, but no matter what the situation may be, these men listen with compassion as others share their needs.

My Future

In my immediate future, my eighth decade, I will move out to the cutting edge of my life and develop, facilitate and lead more training and growth events. If I can train others in the insights and methods that have shaped me, God's work will continue through those that I train, just as I carry on the work of those who trained me. This is the kind of work I see myself doing in the future; it is a growing edge for me to develop modules of instruction for this type of work. For example, I believe that I can train others to lead divorce recovery groups. Divorce precipitates so many changes in the life of divorcees. It is a particularly difficult time for all who are involved, and a person with compassion and training can help people through these tough times.

Every emotionally intense life experience, whether loss of a job, divorce or death, fills people with such anxiety that it often forces them to act out in ways that are destructive to them and to those they love. My training will aim to help my understudies be an influence creating health and hope in people passing through life's crises.

As I stand on the front side of my eighth decade of life, I am postured to the future with beams of hope. The future is a mystery and out of that mystery will emerge the people, the experiences and the challenges that are necessary for me to complete my journey. I do want to walk faithfully on the long journey home. As I face this future, there are some normal, earthy, mundane things that I look forward to. I anticipate an uninterrupted time with Jane when we can reflect on our lives together and the prospects for our future. Sometimes in my busy life, this very important focus gets neglected.

But there are also other members of the family that I want to spend time with. I look forward to being with Jane Gower, her husband and our two grandchildren. I have no other experience that equals seeing my grandchildren growing up and developing healthy habits. I delight to take them to Disney World to see them meet all the comic book characters; what a gleam comes in their eyes when they meet characters they have seen on television. I love to see them walk down the street sucking on a Popsicle or eating ice cream. I love being a grandfather!

With respect to Robert and his continued development, I keep looking forward to his finding the maximum fulfillment of which he is capable. I very much want to stay with him on his journey, and I want not only to journey with Robert but with our granddaughter Madelyn Lane as well. Jane makes trips to Omaha to spend time with Robert and with Madelyn Lane. She is an energetic, bright little girl. Her mother Jodi is caring for her well. Jodi is a good mother and has the love and support of two sisters and her mother in Omaha. I am grateful that Madelyn Lane has the love and support of a caring family.

As I look out into the future, I see the mystery looming on the horizon. I speak of the mystery of God, of homecoming, of moving into the next dimension of my existence. I do not know what that will mean for me. I have read the Bible as it speaks about a heaven that has streets of gold, fountains of water and rivers that flow from the Throne of God. According to the Bible along the river there are trees that produce fruit for the healing of all the nations. This language is highly symbolic; it is rich in metaphor. The golden streets, the strumming harps and the gigantic angels mean something, but the interpretation is mostly hidden from me.

I think heaven will offer the graduate school course in becoming more and more what we were created to be. Perhaps eternity is devoted to our unfolding the potential that God put in us. I don't think that heaven is all in the future; a bit of it touches us here and now. When God said, "Let there be Robby, let there be Jane, let there be Robert, let there be Jane Gower," these persons came into being with God's mark upon them. Though I cannot see beyond the horizon and I do not have the power of discernment to envision and to articulate what the next stage is like, I live in hope. I have hope because of the goodness and faithfulness of God. I am eager to see the unfolding of the last chapters of life and to experience the transition into the beyond. The beyond is already within.

My deepest desire for the future is that in this life I will be able to pass on to the next generation what I have found valuable in life. I am deeply grateful for the journey that I have had and I want to stand in the stream of life and pass on something of value to future generations.

The promise God made to Abraham resonates with me. God said to Abraham that his seed would be as numerous as the grains of sand on the seashore and as many as the stars in the heavens. God made the influence of Abraham to ripple out across the ages. I believe that whatever eternal life may mean, it will include the redemptive ripples that each of us has begun, ripples that will go on when our life here is ended.

Appendix

After writing about the influences that have formed my approach to counseling and training, I thought that it would be a good thing to ask some of the people that I have worked with over the past decade to reflect on my style that they experienced in a group or therapy or training event. It seemed to me that it would be beneficial to me and to those who read my story to be able to see what actually happens in my interaction with people. This is a very personal request to make of people, but when I asked a number of them to help with this project, they were more than willing. Although what was written in these responses cannot be limited to one category, I have related them in this order: Personal Counseling, the Alzheimer's Group, the Caregivers Group, the Divorce Recovery Group, A Companion in Ministry, Co-leading with Robby and Touching All the Bases.

Personal Counseling

Martha's story. When I arrived at Robby's office, I was at the bottom of a deep, hopeless hole. Fortunately, I did have a few years in a support group and a church home, which gave at least an outline of how I should feel.

Robby got an idea of what was going on with me and guided me into areas that were hindering me. For example, I was working for an inadequate salary. He never told me that I had to get a different job, but by having a conversation with him, I saw how being paid a fair wage could change my life. With my financial worries relieved, I could see other things more clearly.

I was NEVER told what to do or how to feel. With gentle, leading questions I was able to find a more peaceful place in my life. Today, even though I am not in crisis, I still visit with Robby so than I can stay on a clear path.

Lucy's story. Robby Carroll has enriched my life for over thirty years. I have known him as a counselor when conflicting personal issues arose preceding and following grief and loss. He ministered to my spiritual challenges when they became prevalent in my life. Also, I have experienced Robby in training which assists me with more confidence in dealing with people with particular problems: dementia and Alzheimer's sufferers, mental and physical illnesses in older adults.

In counseling, he raised questions which prompted me to dig deeply into my soul to find answers. He didn't give advice, nor did he tell me what to do. Robby created a safe, questioning environment where my personal responsibility was to be true to myself. He helped me "own" my questions, which were a significant part of the puzzle of my life. Through his ministry of counseling and training, Robby's influence has given me the courage to ask tough life questions that affected me, both positively and negatively. His personal honesty about his own life's journey is a testament to his commitment to helping others. I appreciate his expertise, respect, faith, humor and forthright approach to extremely important issues in my life.

Bob's story. My relationship with Robby Carroll goes back a decade when he joined the staff of Shallowford Presbyterian Church as a Parish Associate. I began to avail myself of his counseling services because I was struggling with a great deal of anxiety and stress. I thought if I could remove or reduce the anxiety and stress, my life would become better and I wouldn't drink so much. I did not realize until later that it was the drinking that caused my anxiety and stress.

I felt comfortable talking to Robby because he was in recovery and understood what I was going through much better than I did myself. He was always kind and extremely patient with me, when during therapy sessions I told elaborate stories about myself and what I needed from others to make me happy. My condition continued to deteriorate and finally Robby suggested I go to a rehab facility. I was not inclined to agree, since I didn't think that was necessary and besides, the holidays were coming up. Just before the Christmas holiday, Robby and I met again, this time with my whole family. Robby conducted what I know now was an intervention. I went into treatment on December 24, 2003.

After I got out of treatment, I continued to meet with Robby. He could tell that I had been drinking again, so he tried some tough love and told me he didn't want to see me again until I had not had a drink for at least a week. I said, "Robby, I sure am going to miss you." But eventually the truths that Robby shared with me began to sink in and by the grace of God I was delivered from my obsession for alcohol.

I continued to meet in Robby's office with him and several others who also suffered from addiction. In the spring of 2005, Robby started the Aftercare Program for people who had completed treatment at

Willingway Hospital in Statesboro, Georgia. I came to those weekly sessions and many times I sat by the window in the Fellowship Hall to see if anybody else would come. Many times they didn't.

Over the years Robby has become a good friend and confidant. During my first year of sobriety, I needed a steadying influence. Robby was always there to listen and encourage me. We went on a Shallowford mission trip together to Mexico in 2004 after I had been sober for only a few months. I watched and admired the way he interacted with the other members of the group, always kind and full of laughter. You always know if Robby is around!

I especially noted how he interacted with his son, Robert. He was always kind and gentle, positive and encouraging. This model was something that I needed to see so that I could relate to my own children in a different way. Robby introduced me to Developing Capable People, a program by Stephen Glenn. This technique for interacting with people has been one of the best things I have ever learned. It taught me how to be a better listener and to seek first to understand, and then to be understood. This training has helped me greatly not only in my family but also in other relationships.

Robby is also unflappable. Once during the early worship service at Shallowford, I gave an announcement from the pulpit. When I finished, I gathered up my notes and returned to my pew. Robby then stepped up to the pulpit to deliver the sermon. He looked down and around and seemed a little confused and concerned. Then he just smiled and launched into his sermon. I looked down and only then realized that I had picked up not only my notes, but I had also picked up Robby's sermon! Robby was unfazed and preached a great sermon.

Robby just rolls with the moment. He always talks about being in the moment, not to worry about the future or fret about the past – live the moment. We have no control over either past or future, but we do have a choice in the present. I have learned this lesson, but it requires constant vigilance because it is so easy to slip back into a state of fear and anxiety about things that I have no control over.

I have watched Robby over the years as he has dealt with personal situations that have challenged his ability to focus on the present. He has not only succeeded, but all the while he has maintained a positive outlook and devoted himself to the service of others.

Robby Carroll is an amazing man who lives his Christian faith every day by loving God and serving others. It is a real privilege to know him and call him my friend. I am so grateful for what he has done for me and my family.

Peace.

Carol's story. For over ten years, Robby has been a source of sanity in my "surely I am crazy" life, an encourager when I felt I couldn't go on, and a cheerleader when I was sure I was not good enough. Robby Carroll is a gifted communicator, a compassionate listener, and one willing to be "on the journey" with those who seek his counsel. He is funny, he is dedicated and he is real.

Because Robby always wants the best for those in his care, he gladly shares his knowledge and personal life experiences. He will also offer or suggest additional means of support and education, acknowledging he doesn't have all the answers.

Best of all, Robby is a grace-filled man of God, a shining example of a redeemed life, and a constant witness to the love of Jesus.

The Alzheimer's Group

Ellen's story. I first began to notice that my husband was not functioning well before anyone else imagined that he might have Alzheimer's. Most spouses are the first to notice. Soon after this recognition we made a trip to Italy. My suspicions began to be confirmed on that trip. I noticed that Ted had problems translating the value of a dollar into Italian currency. And when he offered to guide the group, we had a difficult time finding our way under his leadership.

When we returned home, I tried to explain to our friends that I suspected Alzheimer's, but most of them thought I was jumping to false conclusions. After a short period of time, I decided to have him checked out at Emory. The diagnosis confirmed my worst fears. We joined a class in which they were doing a study of persons with Alzheimer's. Feeling that his plight might eventually help someone else with Alzheimer's, Ted had a purpose for living. He found meaning in helping others by his own suffering and loss.

My struggles didn't seem to have much purpose. I felt alone in my pain as I staggered with my questions. I knew that we had an Alzheimer's group that met in our church. Shortly after Gray Norsworthy came to be our pastor, a woman departing worship asked him, "What do I do with a husband that has Alzheimer's?" The pastor didn't know, but he asked Bill Carr, our associate, to look into the matter. His findings gave birth to the Alzheimer's group.

I recall at the first meeting how people were laughing and having a good time before the session began. The group met in the Burney Overton Room. The leader said that we should talk about whatever was on our heart. I heard members of the group describing my feelings so clearly because they too felt fearful, lonely and helpless. In this group we didn't try to tell people what to do with their helplessness; we just listened.

At home things were getting worse: first it was giving up driving, which Ted resented; then, it was giving up walking by himself because he sometimes got lost. Day after day I watched him slip farther and farther down that long memory hill. He got to a place that I could not meet his needs. If he fell, I couldn't lift him; if he got lost, I couldn't find him. My experiences were all reflected in the stories of others in my Alzheimer's group.

After Bill Carr left, Robby Carroll came as our associate and began leading the Alzheimer's group. I think that he has done a great job of helping us, and I also think that the group has enriched his life.

After Ted's death I kept going to the group because I needed support and suggestions that others related. I hope I can offer to someone a listening ear that others offered me; I hope that I can care for them as I have been cared for. Losing someone to Alzheimer's is a painful process, but having others share it with you makes all the difference.

The Caregivers Group

Mary Ellen's story. Robby Carroll is a soul who has listened to and learned from all of the amazing opportunities his life has provided him. He has been able to use all of these life experiences to become a very effective counselor and teacher.

My association with Robby began when he first came to Shallowford and started to lead our lay "Care Ministers" training. Care Ministers are volunteers from the church who stay in touch with our shut-in members or members going through a difficult time. We meet monthly to share what is going on with the folks we're contacting, as well as to learn more effective ways to provide support to these folks.

An ongoing theme in the training Robby provides the Care Ministers is the power and importance of listening. Robby has helped us to recognize that our role is not to "fix" the problem, but to really listen, thus allowing other persons the opportunity to process their situation and come up with solutions that will work for them. He has helped us realize that we all see life through our own lenses that are tinted by our peculiar life experiences. Because we all have our own unique set of life experiences, we can never really "know how someone else feels." He has helped us to believe that one of the most meaningful gifts we can give other people is to fully listen and hear their story. These deep connections with other human beings are an example of how God works through us to demonstrate God's love for all of us.

Because of the training Robby provides the Care Ministers, I believe that more people are able to feel God's love through the caring support of the Care Ministers than could be provided by the church staff alone. The reason I believe Robby to be an effective counselor and teacher is his willingness to share his own vulnerability. He is not afraid to admit that he is not perfect, and therefore I can feel more comfortable sharing my own struggles and weakness. He helps me feel accepted and valued for who I am, just the way I am.

Robby is constantly looking for ways to involve more individuals in service and ministry at our church. He is well aware that when people have the opportunity to serve others, their life becomes more meaningful. In summary, Robby has extended his positive influence well beyond his counseling practice to many others in our church and community by the training and encouragement that he has provided to so many people.

Divorce Recovery Group

Christine's story. My relation with Robby Carroll has been important in my life. It has been such a relief to talk with him and share my fears, concerns and ultimately my gratitude. I have known Robby for almost thirteen years, and I marvel at how wonderful he has been in our supervision and the impact it has made on the Divorce Recovery ministry at Peachtree Presbyterian Church.

Robby has made supervision both interesting and exciting. There is NO doubt in my mind that had it not been for him – the glue – our group would have floundered and possibly disbanded years ago. He continues to teach us in each "teaching moment" as it happens. To be even more specific, he is able to listen to the issues as they come up and then proceed to draw on his vast knowledge and experience derived from reading, reflecting on life and attending seminars. In training he is able to bring forth the exact information that we need to carry back to our small groups so that we can further help our "peeps." I think the biggest take away for me is the question he frequently asks: "What does that bring up in you?" Answering this question makes us more aware that some of the issues in others are our issues too. This wealth of knowledge that comes from Robby is always fresh and therefore keeps us on our toes!

Even though we have used the book Rebuilding When Your Relationship Ends, Robby uses his own insights and experiences to tie us into the book. This helps us continue to use a tool with which we are familiar. Robby keeps us focused with love and grace. I love how he reminds us that God's hand informs how we handle these issues as well; it is not us, but how God uses us as tools to do his work.

On a more personal level, when Robby found out about my situation with Kevin's incarceration, he reached above and beyond what could be expected to help me with this rugged part of my journey. Robby's efforts have been done with grace, love and compassion so rarely found in a therapist and counselor or in many Christians. I am so grateful to have such a friend and mentor. I pray that God will bless Robby Carroll in all that he does. May he be blessed especially with good health in the years to come!

Co-leading with Robby

Kay's story. What a blessing to call Robby Carroll my pastoral counselor, my colleague, and my friend! As I consider all the ways my life has intersected with Robby's through Shallowford Presbyterian Church, memories emerge that include both boundless laughter and healing tears. Powerful moments of vital connection come to mind around teaching and learning with Robby. Vivid images emerge of Robby's warm smile, his twinkling eyes, and his bellowing voice proclaiming, "Hallelujah!!" I can almost feel that warm hug that makes me feel like I'm all wrapped up in God's love. Robby embodies living in the full presence of life, and his enthusiasm is indeed contagious. He brings the energy of "hallelujah" to all that he does, even as he brings a deep humility and gentleness to each encounter.

While I could share personal reflections of Robby as pastoral counselor and friend, I want to share my perspective as a colleague and co-instructor. It has been my unique privilege to work with Robby in developing and co-facilitating educational programs through Shallowford Family Counseling Center. Robby and I share a passion for inviting all people to educational experiences designed to call forth the best in the human spirit. We both feel called to offer experiences that illuminate and cultivate inner resources for healing and wholeness. In my work with Robby I sense a deep congruence and collective intention to tap into life-giving connections that fuel openness and energize our capacity to live as whole human beings. As we accept both our beauty and our brokenness, we discover a spot of grace inside, and we see the real beauty that shines through our brokenness.

Working with Robby is all about the journey, and what a gift to be on the journey with him. When I teach with Robby, we are learning and growing, moment by moment, even as we plan and deliver experiences of learning and growth for others. Robby always invites me to his office to begin the instruction by listening deeply to what's alive in each of us. Robby knows that we teach who we are, so we are able to connect with our own inner teacher even as we connect with one another in conversation. Robby always creates a safe, welcoming space for us to engage. This is one of Robby's God-given gifts, and he uses this gift in all that he does. Whether it's his role as pastoral counselor, therapist, educator, or friend, Robby opens his heart and listens deeply. The process is life-giving and always offers rich opportunities for both of us to learn and grow as we journey along.

I recall a recent program which focused on parenting; it was a program centered on how to be a parent rather than how to do parenting. As Robby and I did "the work before the work" of facilitating this conversation about the incredible importance of parenting, I observed Robby's authenticity as he embraced his own journey as a father. His wholehearted openness clearly informs his desire to both encourage and support all parents. Robby combines his life experience with his knowledge and experience as a marriage and family therapist, and through this combination he truly embodies the wisdom in the words, "Be the change you wish to see in the world." Robby knows the growth and blessing that is born of pain and brokenness, and he humbly and joyfully reminds me that the point is to love one another in every encounter and to live life in its fullness! When we open our hearts to view life through the lens of grace and love, this allows every experience in life to teach us something. Each moment with Robby teaches me something useful, and to that I say, hallelujah!

Robby Carroll loves life, and teaching alongside Robby is like savoring a delicious meal! Time invested in planning, teaching, and debriefing our shared experience nourishes me in ways that are far beyond words. Robby and I know that we teach who we are. . .and with Robby that's a very good thing! As we often remind one another, it's NOT about the outcome, it's about the process. It's about the journey.

As Robby often says when speaking of our work and our relationships, it's all an "inside job." This wise reminder is reflected in one of Robby's mantras, the Serenity Prayer. Robby lives by this prayer, and he reminds me to live by it, too. . .*accepting the things we cannot change, finding the courage to change the things we can, and seeking the wisdom to know the difference.* Robby inspires me to see what is possible when we accept hardship as a pathway to peace, and he embodies the joy and serenity that can be found in all things. Robby reflects God's grace in a grace-hungry world, and it is a blessing to be on the journey with him!

Hallelujah!

A Companion in Ministry

Tom's story. I am truly thankful for Robby Carroll and for his ministry. Robby has been for me a therapist, church consultant, a friend and a companion in ministry for more than twenty years. I first met Robby through my wife, Lynn, who was in supervision with Robby as the AACPE Supervisor for her license as a Marriage and Family Therapist. From that initial association, I began a counseling relationship with Robby for weekly consultation for normal problems and struggles in pastoring a local congregation. Somehow no matter how discouraged, confused or frustrated I was when I arrived to talk with Robby, by the end of our time together, I had gained a new perspective and the hope to deal with my circumstances again. During one difficult season in which there was a sexual misconduct charge leveled at a member of my staff, Robby not only helped me cope with the stressful interpersonal dynamics, but also gave me wisdom in using the resources of the Presbytery. He supported me through this difficult time and provided me a true confidant as I labored to heal the congregation.

Having a heart for the PCUSA, always yearning for renewal and revitalization, I sought helpful resources wherever I could find them. At times, my searching took me to resources beyond the denomination, to mega-churches, charismatic groups, and worshiping communities of all shapes and sizes. Robby not only affirmed my search, but shared this yearning with me. Thus, over time, Robby and I have had many conversations about calling and future ministry. Robby helped me realize the gifts I possessed for church renewal and/or for new church development and encouraged and affirmed God's call for me. Once I embarked on the adventure of organizing a new congregation, Robby was a continual partner for new church strategy.

While never serving "on staff" at either of the churches I have pastored, Robby has always functioned as a "staff therapist" for members of my congregations. Over the years many of my church attendees and members have found Robby to be helpful in working through any number of personal and work-related challenges. When I have faced difficult issues, especially those with drug addiction, Robby's expertise has been invaluable help to guide members and me.

On other occasions, Robby has actually worked with my leaders to help them envision and plan for the future, leading "visioning" events and helping us work toward healthy solutions in specific areas of conflict and difficulty. In more recent days of ministry, I consult with Robby on an "as needed" basis, and Robby has been gracious to be available to me. Sometimes pastors simply need a place to talk, to cry, to confess, to rant, and Robby Carroll has been and remains that constant, trustworthy person for me. I am so thankful for him!

Touching All the Bases

A number of friends were kind enough to respond to the ways that I have worked with the membership at Shallowford Presbyterian Church and beyond. In one instance a person that I have been very close to for nearly a decade touched all the bases of my type of work. She wrote about her journey to Shallowford Presbyterian Church, her experience with the Alzheimer's Group, becoming an elder in the church, serving communion with one of the ministers, belonging to the Caregivers Group, personal counseling and a relationship with a minister. This response provides a positive summary of what I could only hope to offer people in my role as a counselor, teacher and friend.

Here is **CharleAnn's story**.

Journey to Shallowford Presbyterian Church. As a child, I was raised in the First Baptist Church of Erwin, Tennessee: Sunday school, Vacation Bible School, Sunbeams, and church services. When I look back, it seems so restrictive. For example, my father was a member of the First Christian Church, but after teaching Sunday school classes at First Baptist, he was told he had to be re-baptized in the Baptist church. He didn't participate in church after that. To take communion, one had to be a member of the Baptist church, so I never took communion. My first experience with a Presbyterian church was in Warm Springs, Virginia where I had my first teaching position. At communion the minister said we were coming to Christ's table, and all were welcome. I took communion - with real wine!

When I came to Atlanta in 1972, I visited a number of churches. None felt "right." In 2003, two days after retiring from a thirty-one year teaching career, I became my mother's caregiver. Within months, she was diagnosed with Alzheimer's. On the advice of a stranger (or guardian angel) at T.J. Maxx, I attended the Alzheimer's support group at Shallowford. On leaving the meeting, several young folks recognized me from Lakeside High School, hugged me, and welcomed me to Shallowford. Within a year, I was baptized and became a member. Shallowford has become my family.

Alzheimer's support group. So, it was through the Alzheimer's group that I met Robby Carroll when he became the moderator of the group. When my mother was diagnosed, I knew little about the disease. I've compared it to walking into a totally dark room with blinders on: you don't know where anything is, you bump into a rocking chair, you stumble over tables, you break a vase, and you fall. The group was for me like candles being lit, one at a time. I found my way through Alzheimer's with the love, care, information, and advice from our group.

I cared for Mother in my home for four years. Then, in 2007, she fell, broke her hip, and never regained mobility. She went to assisted living and to a nursing home. It was through these years that Robby was of such spiritual grace to me. He brought a beautiful, pink prayer shawl to Mother when she was first at A.G. Rhodes. He came several times to The Court at Decatur and Fountainview, giving her communion and anointing her with oil. When she suffered a horrible accident at Fountainview, I called Robby from the Emergency Room at Emory requesting his and the church's prayers. On January 15, 2011, Mother passed away, and on February 16, 2011 (it would have been her 89th birthday), Robby officiated at her memorial service. Throughout those years, Robby heard what I said, and what I didn't say, because he heard with his heart.

Elder at Shallowford. Within the first year of my being a member at Shallowford, our pastor, Gray Norsworthy, asked if I'd consider being an elder on session. I was shocked and deeply honored to become an elder. While I was serving on the session, our church was shaken by two events: the firing of our director of children's services, and the resignation of Dr. Norsworthy following his sabbatical. Robby heard with his heart that our church was hurting. He took on the job as Head of Staff with all the responsibilities it involved. I believe Robby's "people skills" held our church together, rather like wrapping all of us in a prayer shawl, giving us spiritual warmth and assurance that all would work out. I witnessed in session meetings his leadership capabilities and ability to compromise in difficult situations. I nominated Robby for a leadership award in an event sponsored by Lynn and Bob Turknett.

Serving Communion. One of the greatest honors for me as an elder has been to accompany the pastor to give communion to shut-ins. Robby, with the simplicity of a roll and grape juice, takes you in prayer to Christ's table with the disciples. He and I have served many folks. One of our dearest is Margaret: 90ish, tiny, and feisty; she is always delighted to see and hug Robby. A member of our Alzheimer's support group, Pat, requested communion after being hospitalized and losing her mother and brother. She died a few months later, and Robby officiated at her memorial service. When my dearest friend, Wanda, was undergoing chemotherapy, we shared communion with her in her home. She passed away in November 2011, and Robby officiated at her funeral service. My former husband, Fred, has suffered several serious health issues within the last six years. Robby and I have taken a prayer shawl and communion to him. In March 2012, Fred had a double aortic thoracic bypass, and one night, he wasn't doing well. I called Robby asking for his prayers, and within an hour, Robby was by Fred's bedside at St. Joseph Hospital. Beyond the boundaries of Shallowford Presbyterian Church, Robby hears with his heart.

Caregivers Group. We have a Caregivers Group at Shallowford. The purpose is to stay in touch with folks who may be shut-ins, who've recently experienced a death in the family, and for those who just need a friendly face and voice. We meet the last Sunday of every month with Robby sharing his wisdom of how to genuinely listen and hear what is said... and not said. We learn that we don't have to "fix" problems, or share our ideas or experiences... just listen. We share our concerns about "our people." There is extraordinary empathy and understanding within the group.

I stay in contact with three senior neighbors: two gentlemen who have lost their wives, and Margaret, the feisty delight.

Personal Counseling. What an incredible blessing to have Robby, an educated therapist and pastoral counselor, at Shallowford. I have talked with Robby a few times over the years regarding some relationship issues. In June 2013, I began a fairly regular schedule of meeting with him. These began after my former husband, Fred, had been seriously ill with gastritis and hospitalized for three weeks. Because his vision, hearing, and mobility are impaired, I had been spending from six to eight hours a day with him, to answer questions from doctors, nurses, therapists, and also to give him some degree of security. By the time he was dismissed, I think I was close to a nervous breakdown. My first session with Robby was spent crying. As we continued talking, I opened up about my marriage and the verbal abuse I'd suffered. More and more, I was able to see a pattern: because of a comment my father made when I was four years old, I didn't feel "good enough" and had developed a pattern of trying to please others. Wow! What an eye-opener! I am becoming stronger, have set boundaries, and realized that the only person I must please is me. Robby listened to me with his heart.

A Personal Relationship with a Minister. I've never had a personal relationship with a minister before. To me, a minister is two notches below an angel! I've established a friendship with Robby because he's real; he's led a life that hasn't been blue skies and red roses. Robby will share that he has experienced clouds, storms, and thorns in his life and along the path to being called to the ministry. When he preaches, he doesn't read from a prepared text; no, he preaches from his heart, walking around, and sprinkling humor in his sermon. If he's an angel, his halo is slightly tilted!

Hallelujah!

Cover art oil painting Jane H. Carroll